Cultural and Political Aspects of NEPAL-CHINA RELATIONS

Vijay Kumar Manandhar

M.A. (T.U.), M.A. (Wisconsin), Ph.D. (T.U.)
Associate Professor
Central Department of History
Tribhuvan University, Kirtipur
Kathmandu, Nepal

Adroit Publishers
Delhi

1999

Reprint, 2007

Cultural and Political Aspects
of
NEPAL-CHINA RELATIONS

Ist Edition : 1999
ISBN : 81-87392-06-1

Published by :
Adroit Publishers
C-8/2, Yamuna Vihar,
Delhi - 110053

Laser Typesetting by :
Krishna Kumar Thapa
Kirtipur, Kathmandu, Nepal

Price : Rs. 595/-

Printed at : Nice Printing Press.

To

My Parents and Teachers

Foreword

Much ink has been spilled in writing about Nepal-British India relations. Although we have multidimensional relations with India since the dawn of history, no substantial work has come out about the subject prior to the British rule in India. Moreover, most of the books on the subject were written by foreigners from their own perspective. As such not much justice has been done to the subject.

Nepal, being situated between two big countries with two different cultures has its multidimensional relations with both. Due to easy access and geographical proximity we have had more interaction with the South than the North. Yet we have close relations with the North i.e. China since long. The Chinese sources so far available refer to the visit of Tseng-tsai (265-420 A.D.) to Nepal-Lumbini and his description about the lapis lazulli image at Lumbini, the birthplace of Lord Buddha, is an important information to us.

We have multi-faceted relations i.e. social, cultural economic and political with China since age long. Tibet is a gateway to reach China. Moreover Nepalese dealt China with dignity to have a strong commercial footing in Tibet for which Tibetans developed a strong dislike and created hurdles. The Nepalese had understood it well. So they handled the situation in a diplomatic way. But generally Nepalese stood beside China when a conflict arose between China and Tibet.

Nepalese interest seems to have changed with the time, situation and the ruling families also. Unfortunately, we have shortage of local sources to deal with Nepal-China relations of the ancient and medieval periods. Whatever materials we have about the subject, we have only the Chinese and Tibetan sources, because of which many questions remain unanswered. For example, why did the Chinese rulers contact the

RamaVardhan family (feudatory of the Malla Kings) instead of the Malla Kings themselves ? Why did Kublai Khan not contact the King of Nepal inspite of being impressed so much by artist Arniko ? Who was Arniko ? Who was Bhrikuti ? Why are the Nepalese sources silent about Bhrikuti ? Why do the 12th/13th Century Chronicles of Tibet only refer to Bhrikuti ? Why are Hiuen Tsang, Wang Hiuen-Tse, Li-i-Piao, the 7th Century Chinese travellers, silent about Bhrikuti ?

Up to this time, we come across multidimensional impact of the Chinese culture in Nepal. Nepalese contributions in art and architecture of China are still in existence. Up to the Nepal-Tibet-China war of 1791-1792, Nepal's political relation with China was an irregular feature. With the signing of the Betravati treaty of 1792, Nepal considered regular political relations with China-- the then Super Power of Asia, a must to have a strong grip on Tibet especially for the lucrative and brisk trade and huge profit therefrom. Based on that feeling and interest, Nepal-China relation was a token of amity, politeness and hospitality and not that of a "tributary" and "suzerain power". Never in the history of Nepal any ruler wished to be a tributary or accept any foreign power as a suzerain power. Any interpretation that nearness to British India could mean total subjugation of Nepal is also absolutely wrong. Dealing with big neighbours by a small nation is really a Herculean task. Moreover, personal interest and ignorance of the rulers also make room for different interpretations. Nepal's relation with China is more marked by amity, hospitality and cordiality on the part of Nepal, although China tried to interpret it otherwise at times.

On this subject my student cum colleague Dr. Vijay Kumar Manandhar, Associate Professor of History, Central Department of History, Tribhuvan University, has been engaged in sincere and indepth studies most meticulously on Nepal-China relations. The present volume, a compilation of twelve research articles (ten published in renowned journals and two unpublished), bears testimony to the author's scholarship.

Indepth research on Nepal-China relation demands thorough knowledge of the Chinese language. But Dr. Manandhar has minimised the shortcoming by studying authentic sources either translated into English by authorative scholars or the archival documents available in National Archives of India, Foreign Ministry Archives of Nepal and National Archives of Nepal.

The first article deals with the first Nepalese Buddhist scholar Buddhabhadra's academic contributions in China in the 5th century. His fifteen so far known academic works are still available in China. He had also worked with Fahsien in the translation of *Mahaparinirvan Sutra* in the Chinese language.

The second group of articles (two) deal with the Chinese Patents to Nepal-one dated March 5, 1789 conferring the titles of "Ertini Wang" on King Rana Bahadur Shah and "Kung" on regent Bahadur Shah by Chinese Emperor Chien Lung and other dated July 5, 1870 offering the title of "Thong-Lin-Pimma-Kokang-Wang-Syang" to Jang Bahadur, the first Rana Prime Minister. Dr. Manandhar has also referred to Chinese claim of her suzerainty over Nepal in 1910. He has approached the Chinese claim analytically and proved the claim as baseless. The Rana Prime Ministers' ignorance and vainglorious pride in getting the title and the staunch nationalistic stand of Prime Minister Chandra Shamsher are presented nicely in the book.

Another group of articles (two) deal with *Kazi* Bhairab Bahadur Gadhatola Kshetri -- Nepalese envoy to China. The first deals with the misdemeanour of the Chinese officials to the Nepalese envoy because of the latter's possession and sale of opium, the contraband object in the erstwhile China. It is a misfortune of Nepal that such an important mission intended to maintain relation with China was misused for personal financial benefit. Another article is an account of the alleged dementia of *Kazi* Bhairab Bahadur. Such behaviour of the envoy seems to result from his failure to dispose of opium sent by the Ranas including the Prime Minister and also Chandra Shamsher's dual policy i.e. sending Mr. Kshetri as envoy and using the second man of the mission as a counterweight to the envoy. Dr. Manandhar has rightly explained those aspects.

The author's understanding of Nepal-China relations is also corresponded by the two articles relating to the employment of a few ex-British Gorkhas and People of mixed Nepalese-Tibetan Ancestry in the Chinese army.

Republic China's four political missions of 1930, 1932, 1934 and 1946 are congenially explained. China's attempt to woo Nepal in its favour is well proved by the missions.

Chinese diplomatic moves made by Manchu dynasty, Chiang Kai-Shek and Mao Tse-Tung to bring Nepal under the Chinese hegemony and efforts made by the Rana Prime Ministers to encounter them successfully are very well analysed.

Dr. Manandhar has very convincingly dealt with the political status of Nepal *vis-a-vis* China.

To conclude, Dr. Manandhar has made a commendable job in bringing out this scholarly work which has expanded the horizon of knowledge of the learned readers. It is expected to provoke new ideas on the subject.

I wish Dr. Manandhar will continue working on the subject to enlighten the enthusiastic and inquisitive scholars. The present work really throws new light on the subject, on which more multidimensional research is further anticipated.

July 23, 1999

Prof. Dr. Tulasi Ram Vaidya

Head, Central Department of History
Tribhuvan University
Kirtipur, Kathmandu, Nepal

Foreword

During the last two decades, a number of works have been published on the Nepal-Tibet relations, but the material is still lacking on Nepal-China relations. In this context, I am happy to see the papers by Dr. Vijay Kumar Manandhar on the different aspects of relations between Nepal and China printed in a book form. Most of these papers have been previously appeared in different journals and magazines, while a few are still unpublished, and the readers get an opportunity to study these scattered papers in a single volume.

As regards the subject matter of these papers, they can be broadly divided into six streams viz. cultural interaction, Chinese Patents to Nepali rulers, Nepal's five yearly missions and the question of opium trade, Chinese enlistment of the Nepali Warriors, the Chinese missions of the 1930s and 1940s, and the political status of Nepal *vis-a-vis* China.

All these papers have been prepared on the basis of original unpublished documents, especially those preserved in the National Archives of India. The documents from the Ministry of Foreign Affairs, Nepal, National Archives of Nepal, and Royal Nepal Army Headquarters have also been used, but they are very few.

While analyzing the Chinese patents, the author aptly writes how it became an excuse for China to claim her suzerainty over Nepal in 1910; through the papers on Nepali missions he has unearthed many new facts; and the subject matter of the Chinese missions between the years 1930 and 1946 is almost new to the general readers. On the political status of Nepal, the author is correct to say that "Nepal's so-called tributary relationship with China from the political and legal point of view seemed less real and more psychological".

On the Chinese intrigues against Nepal, the author describes how the events of 1913 relating to Chinese intrigues against Nepal put the official relations between the two countries at the lowest ebb till 1955. Perhaps, the only limitation of the book is the descriptive style of presenting the themes and issues, which need more analyses and comments than a mere description. With the hope that the author will make full use of his scholarship in the next edition, I congratulate him for his valuable contribution to the study of cultural and political aspects of Nepal-China relations.

July 25, 1999

Dr. Tri Ratna Manandhar

Professor of History
&
Dean
Faculty of Humanities & Social Sciences
Tribhuvan University
Kirtipur, Kathmandu, Nepal

Preface

This book is a collection of twelve articles mainly dealing with the different aspects (phases) of Nepal-China relations. Of the twelve articles, two are unpublished, and the remaining ten articles were published in the Research Journals -- *Voice of History, Rolamba* and *Journal of Nepalese Studies*. Most of them were written from 1995-1998. Only one article is from 1986.

In spite of the fact that Nepal and China have a long history of political and cultural relations, until this time, no thorough research has been done on Nepal-China relations from the time of their inception until the 1950s. In fact, Nepal-India relations have been a subject of exhaustive studies for research scholars, and to some extent Nepal-Tibet relations have also drawn their attention, whereas Sino-Nepalese relations from their earliest times until the 1950s have been virtually untouched. In view of this fact, this study has been undertaken in order to trace the different dimensions of Nepal-China relations from ancient times until the 1940s. The main objective of compiling these articles into one book is to make the articles published in various Research journals available in one book for interested readers.

The first article is about Buddhabhadra, a prominent Nepalese Buddhist scholar who laid the foundation for Nepal's cultural relations with China in 5th century A.D.. The Nepalese mission of 1789 to China and the important Chinese Patent of 5 March, 1790, which sheds new light on Nepal-China relations, is the subject of the second topic. The third one discusses the Chinese Patent of 5 July, 1870 conferred a Chinese title from Emperor T'ung Chih upon Prime Minister Jang Bahadur Rana and China's claim of suzerainty over Nepal on the basis of the conferment of the said Chinese title upon Jang Bahadur and successive Rana Prime Ministers. The next two articles mainly focus on *Kazi* Bhairab Bahadur's Mission to China in 1906 and the alleged dementia of *Kazi* Bhairab Bahadur during his return journey to Nepal in 1909. The sixth article traces the history of the involvement of the Nepalese Quinquennial missions to China in the opium trade from 1852 to 1906. The seventh one provides the new information about the enlistment of people of mixed Nepalese-Tibetan ancestry by China for the latter's military service. The eighth topic sheds new light on China's recruitment of Ex-Gurkha soldiers in Yunan in 1911. The next two subjects deal exclusively with the Chinese missions of 1930 and 1932 to Nepal and the Chinese missions of 1934 and 1946 to Nepal, based upon rarely used Chinese sources as well as other Nepalese and Western sources. The eleventh one examines Republic China's intrigues against Nepal in 1913. The last article contains the much discussed question of the political status of Nepal *vis-a-vis* China.

This work (study) is mainly based on unpublished original documents preserved in the National Archives of India, New Delhi; the Ministry of Foreign Affairs, Kathmandu; National Archives of Nepal, Kathmandu; and Royal Nepal Army Headquarters, Kathmandu. Relevant books, articles and published documents are utilised at proper places.

With few exceptions, most of the published articles in this compilation have been reproduced intact with only a few minor changes (minor corrections and editing changes). The author takes this opportunity to express thanks to the editors and publishers of *Voice of History, Rolamba* and *Journal of Nepalese Studies* for their kind permission to reprint the articles which appeared in their publications.

I express my sincere appreciation to my esteemed teachers Prof. Dr. Tulasi Ram Vaidya, Head, Central Department of History, Tribhuvan University, Kirtipur, Nepal and Prof. Dr. Tri Ratna Manandhar, Dean, Faculty of Humanities and Social Sciences, Tribhuvan University, for their incessant encouragement, valuable suggestions and for writing scholarly forewards as well. I am profoundly grateful to Prof. Dr. Prem Raman Uprety, Former Head, Central Department of History, T.U., Prof. Dr. Tirtha Prasad Mishra, Executive Director, CNAS, T.U., Historian Hari Ram Joshi, and my colleagues Dr. Shanker Thapa and Bhaveshwar Pangeni for their valuable help and co-operation. I owe a particular debt of gratitude to Millicent Alyssa Pugh for her painstaking proofreading of the manuscript and to Mr. Krishna Kumar Thapa for typing the manuscript. I also wish to express my thanks to the Indian Council of Historical Research, New Delhi and to the concerned staff of the National Archives of India, New Delhi; National Archives of Nepal, Kathmandu; and the Royal Nepal Army Head-Quarters, Kathmandu for their kind assistance with my research work. I also express my profound thanks to Adriot Publications for taking great pains to publish this book. Finally I wish to express my special appreciation to my wife Rupa Manandhar for her untiring efforts and inspiration in writing this book.

Needless to say, the individuals mentioned above are not responsible for the views, interpretations, and misinterpretations that appear in the following pages. All errors of fact and judgement are my own. Healthy criticism and suggestions are always welcome.

Satdobato, Lalitpur, Nepal
July 20, 1999 **Vijay Kumar Manandhar**

Abbreviations

Bikram Sambat	B.S.
Ministry of Foreign Affairs, Kathmandu	MFA
National Archives of India, New Delhi	NAI
National Archives of Nepal, Kathmandu	NAN
Royal Nepal Army Head-quarters	RNAH

Contents

Buddhabhadra: A Prominent Nepalese Buddhist Scholar in China*

Nepal and China have a long history of cultural and political relations. The first recorded official relations between Nepal and China date from the middle of the seventh century A.D., although unofficial contacts between the two countries began in the fifth century A.D. through cultural delegations. Nepal-China cultural relations began through Buddhism which was also a common ground for intellectual and spiritual interest, and intercourse and interaction between Nepal and China. Some of the most prominent figures who immortalized Nepal-China relations are Fa-hsien, Hsuan-tsang, Wang Hsuan-Tse, Buddhabhadra and Arniko. Among them, Buddhabhadra, a prominent Nepalese Buddhist scholar and proponent, has not yet received the proper attention from scholars that he deserves. Hence an attempt is made here to deal with the contributions of Buddhabhadra.

One of the most significant events in the history of Nepal-China cultural relations was the introduction of Buddhism into China in 67 A.D. After their rise two power in the fourth century, the Emperors of the Tsin dynasty worked to promote Buddhist ideals by constructing monasteries. The fifth century was also a remarkable period in the history of Nepal-China cultural relations as it witnessed a marshalling of activities designed to promote Buddhism on the part of Nepalese and Chinese monk-scholars. Here it should be pointed out that

---

* Published in *Rolamba*, Vol. 17, No. 1 (January-March 1997), pp. 8-12.

following the introduction of Buddhism in China, the Buddhist community in China faced several problems – (a) the translation of Buddhist texts with their highly technical terminology, (b) confusion caused by erroneous translation of the Buddhist texts, (c) the misunderstanding of subtle and mystic ideas in Buddhist philosophy, and (d) a lack of disciplinary codes for monastic life. As a result, the Chinese monk-scholars were prompted to undertake hazardous voyages to the Buddhist holy lands of Nepal and India to collect complete and purer sources in order to enrich the Buddhist literature in their homeland. This led to the visits of renowned pilgrim turned monk-scholars Fa-hsien and Hsuan-tsang to Nepal and India in search of genuine texts and the true doctrines and to pay homage to the far-famed Buddhist holy places.

Some of the important features of Nepal-China cultural relations were that it was established by the selfless Buddhist monk-scholars of both Nepal and China, who promised to carry the message of love which Lord Buddha delivered for the emancipation from suffering of mankind. The cultural intercourse between the two countries was mainly initiated by the Chinese. For this reason, source materials concerning its history are to be found in Chinese only. Unfortunately, Nepalese have not recorded the great accomplishments of the prominent Nepalese Buddhist scholar Buddhabhadra, who went to China with a purely missionary spirit and whose name is interwoven with the history of Buddhism in China. Buddhabhadra was indeed the torch-bearer of Nepalese civilization abroad. Significantly, the Chinese have not only preserved the name of this Nepalese Buddhist scholar, but also have preserved the records of the Chinese Buddhist monk-scholars Fa-hsien, Hsuan-tsang, Seng-tsai[1] and others who went to Nepal. These

---

1 Till now, the name of Seng-tsai has not yet received due attention from scholars. This *Yueh Chih* monk of the Tsin dynasty (265-420 A.D.) had not only visited Nepal but had also written "Wuo-Kuo-Shih" (Matters concerning the Foreign Kingdoms). Apart from the fragments of his work which are included in the "Shui-Ching-Chu" (Commentary on the

source materials of spiritual and cultural intercourse between the two countries have not yet been fully explored.

The discovery of four monuments, called Black Dragon Spring in Yanchow, near Nanking in the Kiangsu province of China, has revealed that a Nepalese Buddhist scholar Buddhabhadra[2] visited China in the fifth century A.D.. It is quite interesting to note that with few exceptions, almost all the writers have presented Buddhabhadara as an Indian rather than a Nepalese Buddhist scholar[3]. In fact, Buddhabhadra was not

---

Water Classic), there are some quotations in the "Yuan-Chien-lei-han" (The Ch'ing Encyclopaedia of 1710) as well . His work provides us with an interesting description of Kapilavastu, including an important source of information on the topography of Lumbini, the birthplace of Lord Buddha. Seng-tsai's work was older than the account of Fa-hsien. For the details of Seng-tsai, see L. Petech, *Northern India according to the Shui-Ching-Chu,* Rome: Instituto Poligrafico Dello Stato Piazza Verdi, 1950, p. 6 and pp. 33-40.

2 Rishikesh Shaha, *Heroes and Builders of Nepal,* London: Oxford University Press, 1965, p. 41.

3 Most Nepalese writers, including Chinese and English scholars, have presented Buddhabhadra as a Nepalese Buddhist scholar. Niranjan Bhattarai, *Chin Ra Tyasasita Nepal Ko Sambandha* (China and her relations with Nepal), Kathmandu: Royal Nepal Academy, 2018 B.S., p. 65; Satya Mohan Joshi, *Kalakar Arniko* (Architect Arniko), Kathmandu: Bijay Gajananda Vaidya, 2044 B.S., p. 2; Kaiser Bahadur K.C., *The Judicial Customs of Nepal*, Part I, Kathmandu: Ratna Pustak Bhandar, 1971, p. 138; Jnanmani Nepal, *Nepal Nirukta* (Nepal Indentified), Kathmandu: Royal Nepal Academy, 2041 B.S., pp. 155-156; Pu-Chu Chao, *Buddhism in China* , Peking: Chinese Buddhist Association, 1957, p. 6; Huang Sheng-Chang, "China and Nepal", *People's China,* May 1, 1956, p. 8; T.R Ghoble, *China-Nepal Relations and India*, New Delhi: Deep and Deep Publications, 1986, p. 17; Holmes Welch, *Buddhism Under Mao,* Cambridge, Massachusetts: Harvard University Press, 1972, p. 172; and E. Zur-Cher, *The Buddhist Conquest of China*, Vol II, Leiden: E.J. Brill, 1972, p. 400, Note 236.

Some other writers have described Buddhabhadra as an Indian Buddhist scholar. Jawaharlal Nehru, *The Discovery of India*, London: Meridian Books Limited, 1960, p. 193; Chin Keh-mu, *A Short History of Sino-Indian Friendship*, Calcutta: 1981, p. 54; and Samuel Beal

only the first Nepalese to go to China and to devote his whole life to serving the Chinese people, but also one of the great Buddhist scholars of Nepal who worked for the promotion of Buddhism in Kashmir and China. As such, it is appropriate here to give a short biography of Buddhabhadra. The Chinese transliteration of his name is Fo-t'o-po-t'o-lo[4] and was translated as Chueh-hsien[5]. Although his family was originally from the western part of Nepal, Kapilavastu, the home town of Lord Buddha, they had settled in Nagarahara[6] (the modern Jalalabad in Afghanistan) where Buddhabhadra was born in 358 A.D.. According to one tradition, he is said to have been born as a member of the Shakya family which claimed descent from King Amrtodana, an uncle of Lord Buddha[7]. Having lost his parents at the age of five, Buddhabhadra, along with his grandparents moved from Nagarahara to Kapilavastu, but his grandparents also died soon thereafter. Left an orphan at an early age, some kindhearted people took care of him and Buddhabhadra was admitted to the Buddhist Order. From his very childhood, he had taken interest in Buddhism. By the time he completed his studies at the age of seventeen, he had acquired a profound knowledge of Buddhism. It was said that even at an early age, he read a

---

(ed.), *Buddhist Records of the Western World*, Delhi: Oriental Book Reprint Corporation, Reprint, 1983, p. XII.

4 Prabodh Chandra Bagchi, *India and China*: A thousand years of Cultural relations, Second Edition, New York: Philosophical Library, 1951, Beal, f.n. no. 3, p. 331.

5 Bhattarai, f.n. no. 3, p. 66; Joshi, f.n. no. 3, p. 3; Wang Hung-Wi, "*Chin-Nepal Maitri, Prachin Tara Naulo Utsah Sahitko*" (Ancient China-Nepal Ties but with new enthusiasm), *Smarika* (Souvenir), Kathmandu: Nepal China Maitri Sangh, 2041 B.S., p. 86 and Daisaku Ikeda, *The Flower of Chinese Buddhism*, Tokyo: Whitchall, 1989, p. 81.

6 But according to one tradition, he is said to have born at Kapilavastu. Zur-Cher, f.n.no. 3, p. 400, Note 236.

7 *Ibid.*, Sarat Chandra Das, *Indian Pandits in the Land of Snow*, Calcutta: Firma K.L. Mukhopadhyay, Reprint, 1965, p. 32 and R.C. Majumdar, *The Classical Age*, Bombay: Bharatiya Vidya Bhawan, 1962, pp. 610-611.

thousand words of the scriptures daily [8]. His teachers also gave him a very good and in depth knowledge of Buddhism. As he became a very talented and learned scholar, Buddhabhadra's name became famous in the then Buddhist world. While visiting several Buddhist holy places and Viharas, he came into contact with many Buddhist scholars. During his visits to various Buddhist Viharas, he happened to reach Mauthyan Tholo Vihara of Kashmir, India. At the request of the head of the said Kashmiri Buddhist Vihara, Buddhabhadra remained there and started giving lessons on Buddhism there. He proved to be a talented Buddhist scholar. During that period, Nepal's far-flung reputation as the birthplace of Lord Buddha had attracted the Chinese visitors, who defied the difficulties of climate and terrain in their scholastic zeal and religious fervour. Fa-hsien, the noted Buddhist monk-scholar of Shanshi province, was one of the earliest Chinese pilgrims to visit Nepal and India. Intent on making a thorough study of Buddhism by procuring authentic texts of Buddhist books on monastic discipline and searching for famous Buddhist scholars to bring back with them to China, Fa-hsien, at the advanced age of sixty five, along with four other Chinese monks spent fifteen years in India from 399 to 414.A.D.[9]. The importance of Fa-hsien lies in the fact that he was not only one of the earliest Chinese to enter Nepalese territory, but also helped make the trip of Buddhabhadra, the first Nepalese Buddhist monk-scholar ever to visit China successful [10].

---

8 It was also said that once his fellow-student Sanghadatta, while lost in meditation, once saw Buddhabhadra appear suddenly, and asking him whence he came, he said he had been to the Tushita heaven to see Maitreya, Das, f.n.no. 7, p. 32.

9 Fa-hsien, *A Record of the Buddhist Countries*, Peking: Chinese Buddhist Association, 1957, pp. 50-51; and James Legge, *A Record of Buddhist Kingdoms*, New York: Paragon Book Reprint Corp., Reprint, 1965.

10 While in India, Fa-hsien is said to have met the Nepalese scholar and had decided to translate many of the Classic Buddhist texts into

At the time of Fa-hsien's visit to India, there was another Buddhist party from China, visiting India independently of Fa-hsien. The five member Chinese Buddhist party consisted of Pao-Yun, Che-Yen, Sang-Shao, Hwuy-Keen and Sang-King. Pao-Yun was the leader of this Chinese Buddhist party. During the course of their visit, this five member Chinese Buddhist party came to Kashmir, a prestigious Buddhist centre for learning, where they acquired knowledge of Buddhism. This Chinese delegation, at the time of its departure, requested for the Buddhist community there to send a scholar of repute along with them to China. The head of the Kashmiri Vihara strongly recommended the name of Buddhabhadra, stating that he was not only a descendant of Lord Buddha, but was from the land of Lord Buddha. Moreover, he was a great scholar of Buddhism. Therefore, the Chinese delegation requested for Buddhabhadra to go along with them to China. At first, the Nepalese Buddhist scholar was reluctant to go on the grounds that China was a faraway and completely new and foreign country. But afterwards, following Chinese requests as well as thinking that he could propagate Buddhism in China as well, Buddhabhadra made the decision to go and preach the teachings of Lord Buddha in faraway China. Che-Yen was given credit for inviting Buddhabhadra to China. Buddhabhadra set out for China with these Chinese Buddhist monks in 406 A.D.. While making the over-land journey towards China from India, they crossed six countries and faced many difficulties, and reached Vietnam *via* Burma. From there they continued their journey by sea. During their sea-journey towards China, it was reported that Buddhabhadra impressed all his fellow travellers by foretelling the strange events that were to come. At last, they reached the port of Tsingtao of the Chinese province of Shantung in 409 A.D.[11]. From there they went to Ch'ang-an (the modern Sian in

---

Chinese in collaboration with Buddhabhadra, Bhattarai, f.n. no. 3, pp. 65-74; and K.C., f.n. no.3, p. 138.

11 Bhattarai, f.n. no. 3, pp. 68-71. But it seems that some writers have mistakenly referred to Buddhabhadra's arrival in China as having fallen between 389 and 399 A.D.. A.A. Bokshchanin, "Sino-Indian Relations

Shensi province), the then capital of China. Upon their arrival at the Chinese capital, they were greatly welcomed by the Emperor as well as the people of China and were taken to Ch'ang-an's biggest monastery. After his arrival in Ch'ang-an, Buddhabhadra started preaching Buddhism. He solved a lot of puzzling questions regarding Buddhism from Chinese monks who were greatly convinced by his answers. Due to his scholarship, Chinese scholars as well as laymen were greatly influenced. Shortly afterwards, due to doctrinal differences, he came into conflict with Kumarajiva[12], a scholar of great reputation in China. The followers of Kumarajiva fabricated charges against Buddhabhadra[13]. This resulted in the expulsion of Buddhabhadra from Ch'ang-an. In 410 A.D., Buddhabhadra arrived with some forty disciples at Lu-Shan, where Hui-Yuan, the noted Chinese monk-scholar, warmly welcomed the Nepalese Buddhist scholar for his reputation as a *Dhyana* master. Later on, along with his disciples, Buddhabhadra went to Nanking.

Upon his arrival in China in 414 A.D., during his long tour, Fa-hsien was baffled by the dispute between Buddhabhadra and Kumarajiva, so Fa-hsien proceeded to Nanking in order to assuage Buddhabhadra. Later he was successful in persuading the Nepales scholar to return to the capital at Ch'ang-an, where he was warmly welcomed by the

---

from ancient times to the sixteenth century", *China and Her Neighbours*, Moscow: Progress Publishers, 1981, p. 121; Majumdar, f.n. no. 7, pp. 610-611; and Das, f.n. no. 7, p. 32.

12 For sometime Buddhabhadra seemed to have worked together with Kumarajiva. Bhagwatsharan Upadhyaya, *Brihattar Bharat* (Greater India), Delhi: Rajpal and Sons, 1986, p. 163 and Majumdar, f.n. no. 7, pp. 610-611. For the dispute between Buddhabhadra and Kumarajiva, see Kenneth K.S. Ch'en, *Buddhism in China: A Historical Survey*, Princeton, New Jersey: Princeton University Press, 1964, p. 109; E. Zur-Cher, *The Buddhist Conquest of China*, Vol. 1, Leiden: E.J. Brill, 1972, p. 223, and K.C., f.n. no.3, pp. 137-141.

13 It is said that some people, who became very jealous of Buddhabhadra's learning and popularity, tried to defame him by fabricating certain charges. But afterwards, when the truth was revealed, they repented. Bhattarai, f.n. no. 3, pp. 72-75.

Emperor. After remaining for sometime in Ch'ang-an, along with Fa-hsien, Buddhabhadra once again returned to Nanking, where the Nepalese scholar became the senior translator at the Tao Chang Ssu Monastery, giving guidance to more than a hundred monks engaged in putting the Buddhist scriptures into Chinese. This monastery was the main centre of such work in China. While in Nanking, collaborating with Fa-hsien, he started the project of editing and translating several famous Buddhist texts from Sanskrit into Chinese[14]. It is to be noted that by that time, he had acquired a profound knowledge of the Chinese language. Even after Fa-hsien's death in 420 A.D., Buddhabhadra was engaged in translation projects. The Nepalese scholar continued his activities until his death at the age of seventy one in 429 A.D.. Fifteen of his translated works are said to still be preserved in China, the most extensive of which was the *Avatamasaka-Sutra* (Discourse on the Garland) in fifty chapters[15]. This work was completed in 420 A.D.[16]. In 416 A.D., along with Fa-hsien, Buddhabhadra translated *Mahasanghika Vinaya* into forty volumes[17]. The most noted work which Buddhabhadra translated into Chinese in collaboration with Fa-hsien was *Maha-parinirvana-Sutra* (Discourse on the Great Decease) in six volumes[18]. Others

---

14 Chang, f.n. no.3, pp. 8-9 and Legge, f.n. no. 9, pp. 2-3. Here it should be mentioned that Fa-hsien had brought many Classic Buddhist texts from India.

15 Probhat Kumar Mukherjee, *Indian Literature Abroad (China)*, Calcutta: 1928, p. 23, Chou Hsiang-Kuang, *A History of Chinese Buddhism*, Allahabad: Indo-Chinese Literature Publication, 1956, p. 72; Chen, f.n. no. 12, p. 313,note 2; Zur-Cher, f.n. no. 3, p. 407, note 71; Bagchi, f.n. no. 4, p. 205. Fujieda Akira, "The Tun-huang Manuscripts", *Essays on the Sources for Chinese History*, Canberra: Australian National University Press, 1973, p. 123 and Giuseppe Tucci, *The Religions of Tibet*, New Delhi: Allied Publishers Private Limited, 1980, p. 270.

16 P.V. Bapat (Ed.), *2500 Years of Buddhism*, Delhi: The Publications Division, Ministry of Information and Broadcasting, Government of India, 1959, p. 124.

17 *Ibid.*, J.K. Nariman, *Literary History of Sanskrit Buddhism*, Delhi: Motilal Banarsidass, Reprint, 1972, p. 263 and Rahul Sanskrityan, *Baudha Sanskriti* (Buddhist Culture), Calcutta: Adhunik Pustak Bhawan, no date, p. 297.

18 Joshi, f.n. no.3, pp. 2-3.

included the *Vinayapitaka* (the code of monastic discipline) of the Mahasanghik school in thirty four chapters, *Buddha Vatamsaka Mahavaipulya Sutra* in thirty four chapters, *Buddhanusmrti-Samadhi* (a discourse on the contemplation of the Buddha), *Gharva Sutra, Gyan Sutra, Samadhi Sutra, Vaipulya Sutra* and *Manjushree Sutra* of Swear and Vow[19]. Besides Fa-hsien, other Chinese monks Hui-Yuan, Fa-Yeh and a host of other monks were also engaged in Buddhabhadra's translation projects[20]. A large number of Buddhabhadra's works have been mentioned in Samuel Beal's edited book "Catalogue of the Chinese Tripitaka"[21].

Thus we can see that Buddhabhadra's efforts constitute a glorious chapter in the history of mutual exchange among Buddhist cultures. He happened to be one of those important "Scholar-translators" – who had been instrumental in introducing the sacred Buddhist texts into China. Through his translation work, he made an outstanding contribution by propagating Buddhism in China. He also happened to be one of the prominent Buddhist scholars who was invited to stay in the large monasteries of China. He was indeed a person of exceptional status, and his career was typical. It is said that through his efforts, the 'Chan' *(Dhyana)* Sect, a sect dedicated to the meditation teachings of his teacher Buddhasena, was propagated throughout the region south of the Yangtze. In addition to that, he is said to have been responsible for popularising the doctrine of Bhadresvara. In this way, by spending twenty one years in China, he laid a strong foundation for the propagation of the peaceful message of Buddhism in

---

19 Bhattarai, f.n. no. 3, p. 76 and Kaisher Bahadur K.C., "Historical Analysis with Translation into English of the Bi-Lingual Inscription of "Arya Usnisa Vijaya Dharni" Discovered by His Majesty King Mahendra in the Musuem of Sian on Friday, October 6, 1961". *Souvenir*, Kathmandu: Nepal China Cultural Council, 1982, p. 23.

20 Joshi, f.n. no. 3, p. 69.

21 Quoted in Swayambhu Lal Shrestha, *Swayambhu Lal Shresthaya Layaya ChowKhan* (Selected Essays of Swayambhu Lal Shrestha on Nepalese Culture), Part I, Lalitpur: Lok Sahitya Parishad, Nepal Sambat 1106 (2043 B.S.) (In Newari and English), p. 77.

China. The friendship between Nepal and China was a direct outcome of Buddhabhadra's working in partnership with Fa-hsien. For this reason, he can be regarded as one of the most important Nepalese in laying the foundation of Nepal's cultural relations with China. It is also said that Buddhabhadra's name, written in gold letters, is still found in China. Much research still needs to be done on this early immortal Nepalese figure.

***

The Nepalese Mission of 1789 to China and the Chinese Patent of 5 March, 1790*

Nepal-Tibet War of 1788 originated mainly due to the worsening of Nepal-Tibet relations over the question of currency, trans-Himalayan trade, the internal conflict in Tibet which lead to the flight of Shamar Trulku to Nepal in 1788 for political asylum and the expansionist nature of the Nepalese. The Nepalese army invaded Tibet in 1788 and reached Dzongkha and Shekar Dzong, two strategic towns deep inside Tibet, which greatly threatened Tashilhunpo and resulted in the flight of the infant Panchen Lama to Lhasa for safety. At that critical juncture, the Chinese *Amban* (Resident) in Tibet, Shu-lien, reported the matter to the Emperor, which eventually brought the Chinese army into Tibet. It was due to the good overtures of China, that after a long negotiation, Nepal and Tibet signed a treaty at Kerung on 19 July, 1789. Following the signing of the Kerung treaty, Nepal, at the persuasion of the Chinese officials, sent a mission in September 1789 with valuable presents to Ch'ing Emperor Ch'ien Lung, who bestowed titles to King Ran Bahadur Shah and Regent Bahadur Shah through the Patent of 5 March, 1790. In this paper an attempt is made to discuss the 1789 Nepalese mission to China as well as the Chinese Patent of 5 March, 1790 especially this important Chinese Patent of 5 March, 1790, which sheds a new light on Nepal-China relations and surprisingly has not yet been properly discussed by any one so far.

---

* Published in *Rolamba*, Vol. 17, No. 2 (April-June 1997), pp. 11-18.

The Nepalese Mission of 1789 to China

One of the major outcomes of the Nepal-Tibet war of 1788 was the re-establishment of Nepal-China relations after a lapse of nearly four centuries. The Chinese officials General Pa-Chung, Ao-hui and Cheng-teh, who were sent by Chinese Emperor Ch'ien Lung to investigate the situation in Tibet following the outbreak of the Nepal-Tibet war of 1788, informed the Nepalese government that they would settle the matter through their good offices in case the Nepalese government kept friendly relations with the Chinese government by sending a mission to China which involved high officers, with presents as token of friendship. The Nepalese government's acceptance of the Chinese proposal paved the way for the initiation of negotiations between Nepal and Tibet, ultimately leading to the signing of the Kerung treaty of 1789. After the signing of the Kerung treaty, General Pa-Chung, as well as the Chinese *Amban*, seem to have visited Kathmandu. Besides that, there is also the reference to the arrival of the Yang Tingliang mission[1] in the Nepalese capital, which achieved its goal of persuading the Nepalese government to send a Nepalese mission to the Ch'ing Court to receive imperial favours. Knowing the Chinese reaction to the war and the settlement that followed, as well as with the hope that their trade difficulties with Tibet would be eased with the opportunity to by-pass the Chinese authorities in Tibet, Nepal sent a mission under *Kazi* Hari Shahi and Balbhadra Khawas to Peking in September 1789 with a memorial and valuable presents to Emperor Ch'ien Lung[2]. It

---

1 A.S. Martynov, "Some Aspects of Qing Policy in Tibet at the close of the 18th Century", in S.L. Tikhvinsky (ed.), *Manzhou Rule in China*, Moscow: Progress Publishers, 1983, pp. 228-229.

2 Colonel Kirkpatrick, *An Account of the Kingdom of Nepaul*, New Delhi: Asian Educational Services, Reprint, 1986, p. 343. For the

seems that Nepal sent the 1789 Nepalese mission to China for the purpose of establishing friendly intercourse with distant China in order to cultivate the goodwill and friendliness of the Chinese government. It also appears that Nepal despatched the mission to China mainly in order to enforce the 1789 treaty of Kerung on the part of the Tibetans and to safeguard her greater commercial interests in Tibet by securing Chinese recognition of them. The Nepalese presents included tame elephants, foreign horses, an orchestra[3], four complete rolls of Nepalese embroidered stuffs, four silver tea *Samovars* weighing fifty ounces a piece and silver wine beakers of same weight, a pair of cloisonne incense burners and a pair of carved tea-cups[4]. Besides sending presents to the Chinese Emperor, Nepal also sent presents to the Chinese authorities, such as the Chinese *Ambans* of Lhasa, Chinese officials of Digarcha (Shigatse) and Thindafu[5]. For the convenience of the 1789 Nepalese mission, which consisted of twenty-five members[6], Pa-Chung had made arrangements for horses and mules from the Nepal border to Peking, as well as one interpreter and one *Sardar*[7]. The delegation took six months to reach Peking. They were received with full honours by the Ch'ing Court, and remained in the

details of the 1789 Nepalese mission. See Ministry of Foreign Affairs(MFA), Kathmandu, Poka No. Pa 64.

3 Schuyler Cammann, *Trade Through the Himalayas*, Princeton, New Jersey: Princeton University Press, 1951, p. 120.

4 See Appendix A.

5 MFA, Poka No. Pa. 64

6 *Ibid*; and Kirkpatrick, f.n. no. 2, p. 343. But Shakabpa has mentioned that the Nepalese mission consisted of twelve members. See Tsepon W.D. Shakabpa, *Tibet: A Political History*, New Haven: Yale University Press, 1967, pp. 161-162.

7 ChittaRanjan Nepali, "Nepal-Chin Yuddha" (Nepal-China War), *Sharada*, Vol. 21, No. 1, 2013 B.S., p. 204. Kirkpatrick has mentioned that General Pa-Chung sent an *Amban* of his own family with the Nepalese delegation to Peking. Kirkpatrick, f.n. no. 2, p. 343.

Chinese capital for forty five days, during which period Emperor Ch'ien Lung granted them fifteen audiences. The Nepalese delegates presented the gifts from the Nepalese King to the Chinese Emperor, who in return presented more valuable gifts to the Nepalese delegates for presentation to the Nepalese monarch. Emperor Ch'ien Lung also bestowed the Chinese title of "Ertini Wang" on King Ran Bahadur Shah, and the Chinese title of "Kung" on the Regent Bahadur Shah, hoping that Nepal would not be aggressive towards Tibet in the future[8]. Besides the leaders, each member of the 1789 Nepalese mission received official robes and suitable presents from the Chinese Emperor[9] The Nepalese mission spent fourteen months on its journey to and from the Chinese capital.

The importance of the Nepalese mission of 1789 lies in the fact that it was the first Nepalese delegation to visit China after Shakti Singh Rama's mission to the Ming court in 1418, thus establishing direct communication with China after a lapse of nearly four centuries. One of the outcomes of the direct contact between Nepal and China through the 1789 Nepalese mission was the decoration of the Nepalese King with the Chinese title and robes. King Ran Bahadur Shah was the first Nepalese monarch to get the Chinese title of "Ertini Wang", and

---

8 Patent of 5 March, 1790, Foreign Secret E, July 1911, No. 264, National Archives of India, New Delhi (NAI). For the details of the Patent. See Appendix A. Here it should be mentioned that D.R. Regmi and Shakabpa have wrongly stated that it was through the 1792 Nepalese mission to China that Ch'ing Emperor Ch'ien Lung conferred the title of "Wang" and plumes for their Crowns on King Ran Bahadur Shah and Regent Bahadur Shah.
D.R. Regmi, *Modern Nepal*, Vol. I, Calcutta: Firma K.L. Mukhopadhyay, Second Edition, 1975, p. 483 and Shakabpa, f.n. no. 6, p. 169.

9 *Ibid.*

it was continued by his successors up to King Prithvi Bir Bikram Shah.

The Chinese Patent of 5 March, 1790

Here it will not be out of context to mention that by 1910 China started asserting her claim of suzerainty over Nepal. One important basis for the Chinese claim was the Chinese Patent of 5 March, 1790 which bestowed upon King Ran Bahadur Shah the Chinese title of "Ertini Wang". After this, the Nepalese Prime Minister Chandra Shamsher, after consultation with the British Resident in Nepal, J.Manners Smith sent to J.N. Jordan, the British Minister at Peking, the original letter written on the occasion of the conferment of the title of "Ertini Wang" on Nepalese King Ran Bahadur Shah. The Nepalese Prime Minister asked J.N. Jordan to supply a literal translation in English of the Chinese portion of the letter. Upon the receipt of the original letter sent by the Nepalese Prime Minister, J.N. Jordan stated that that letter was written in the Manchu, and not in the Chinese language, and as such it would consequently be a matter of some difficulty to obtain an accurate and reliable translation[10]. Finally, J.N. Jordan sought the help of Edmund Backhouse, a British student of Oriental Languages residing in the city of Peking, who translated the Manchu portion of the Patent conferred by the Ch'ing Emperor on the Nepalese King, and remarked that the translation could be considered to be substantially accurate. The British Minister at Peking remarked that the actual title conferred by the Ch'ing Emperor's Patent was of the type that would be bestowed on the rulers of feudatory states. He also mentioned that the title of "Ertini Wang" conferred on King Ran Bahadur Shah in 1790 may be

10 J.N. Jordan to Govt. of India, 4 February 1911, Foreign Secret E, July 1911, No. 259, NAI.

taken as being equivalent to "Fa Wang" (in Sanskrit *Dharma Raja*) or "Prince of the (Religious) Law", customarily bestowed upon eminent supporters of the Lamaist hierarchy[11]. The translation which the British Minister sent from Peking was not an encouraging one to the Nepalese government. Meanwhile, Prime Minister Chandra Shamsher denied that the Chinese title to the Nepalese King in any way indicated Nepal's feudatory status *vis-a-vis* China. Here, it should be pointed out that only at one time was the Patent of 5 March, 1790 bestowed upon King Ran Bahadur Shah with the Chinese title of "Ertini Wang". Since then, the Chinese government had been applying it indiscriminately with the title of "Wang" to all the successive Kings of Nepal. Interestingly, in spite of not having been formally decorated with this Chinese title, the Nepalese Kings from Girvanyuddha Vikram up to Prithvi Bir Vikram used the term "Wang" for themselves while addressing the Ch'ing Court.

The Chinese Patent of 5 March, 1790 provides us with the following important information on Nepal-China relations. Firstly, it refers to the Nepalese and Chinese governments' viewpoints regarding the causes leading to the Nepal-Tibet war of 1788. The Chinese held that Tibet had increased the rates of private duties on Nepalese merchandise and had unjustly resorted to acts of deceit and treachery against the Nepalese, whereas the Nepalese had stated that the sole cause of Nepal's having entered into hostilities with Tibet was due to Nepal's inability to put up with the Tibetans' acts. The Chinese seemed to have been satisfied with the Nepalese version of the war of 1788. Secondly, the Patent also gives us information regarding the Chinese government's despatching of General Yang Yao to settle the dispute between Nepal and Tibet, as well as China's

11 Same to Same, 7 March 1911, Foreign Secret E, July 1911, No. 264, NAI.

pardoning of Nepal's rash action upon entering into hostilities. China instructed Nepal to withdraw her troops from the Nepal-Tibet border and granted the privilege of transporting private merchandise with the tribute mission to Peking. Thirdly, it also provides us with important facts about the arrival of the Nepalese mission at Peking with memorial and various presents for the Ch'ing Emperor, the receiving of the Nepalese mission with full honours by the Ch'ing Court, which honoured almost all the members of the 1789 Nepalese mission by conferring buttons, coats and robes corresponding to their ranks, as well as by providing suitable presents to them from the Ch'ing Emperor. Most importantly, it also mentions Ch'ing Emperor Ch'ien Lung's having conferred Nepalese King Ran Bahadur Shah with the title of "Ertini Wang" (Prince of the Law), along with a jewelled red button, as was bestowed upon Princes, a court robe, four badges embroidered with dragons, four official mid-length coats; a necklace of 108 beads of amber, a girdle, purse and various fittings to match. Significantly enough, according to the same Chinese Patent, Emperor Ch'ien Lung had also conferred upon King Ran Bahadur Shah's son the Chinese title of "Kung" (The Bravet Rank of a Duke), along with an ordinary coral first class button, a silken robe, a mid-length coat, a necklace of 108 beads of coral, a girdle, purse and appendages. Here it should be mentioned that the Chinese Emperor's having conferred the Chinese title of "Kung" upon King Ran Bahadur Shah's son seems to be far from the truth, for it is a historical fact that King Ran Bahadur Shah's first (eldest) son Ranodyot Shah was born only in 1794. Therefore, it seems quite certain that the Chinese Emperor bestowed the title of "Kung", along with official robes and suitable presents, not to King Ran Bahadur's son, but to King Ran Bahadur Shah's uncle, Bahadur Shah, the Regent of Nepal (1785-1794). It is also evidenced in a document[12] of the Ministry of Foreign Affairs, Kathmandu. Fourthly, the Chinese Patent also mentions the Ch'ing Emperor's instructions to King Ran Bahadur Shah to maintain peaceful relations with the Dalai Lama and Panchen Lama and to observe the existing regulations, to display full reverence and respect for the law, and to maintain its ordinances. Lastly, whatever meaning may have been attached to the 1789 Nepalese mission to Peking by Nepal, the Chinese Patent indicates that the Chinese Emperor, for his part, regarded the 1789 Nepalese mission to China as indicative of the desire, on the part of Nepal, to be included among the tributaries of his Empire. Here it should be pointed out that after inflicting defeat on Tibet and emerging victorious from the Nepal-Tibet war of 1788, Nepal sent a mission to the Ch'ing Court in September 1789 in response to persuasion by Chinese officials which the Ch'ing Court assumed to be a "tributary mission". Upon examining the Chinese sources as quoted by Wei-Yuan and Rockhill[13], it appears that the Ch'ing Emperor Ch'ien Lung was quite misled by his General's report regarding the nature of 1789 Nepalese mission to China, for the Chinese officials gave the Ch'ing Emperor the impression that the Nepalese were offering submission after the Chinese victory. Therefore, General Pa-Chung reported to the Ch'ing Court that the rebels, that is, the Nepalese, had surrendered and that the "Vanquished" Nepalese would bring a tribute, and made careful arrangements to provide them with their own interpreter for the Nepalese mission. He did not inform the Ch'ing court of the terms of the

---

12 Chinese Emperor's *Parwana* (letter, order) to King Ran Bahadur Shah, Chhyalun 55th Year 1st Month, MFA, Poka No. Pa. 64. See Appendix B.

13 Perceval Landon, *Nepal*, Vol. II, Kathmandu: Ratna Pustak Bhandar, Reprint, 1987, pp. 275-282, and W.W. Rockhill, (*The Dalai Lamas of Lhasa and their relations with the Manchu Emperors of China), Toung Pao*, Vol. XI, 1910, p. 51.

1789 Kerung treaty, but just reported that he had obtained a promise from the Nepalese to withdraw from Tibetan territory and never to attack Tibet again[14]. It seems that the Nepalese were not aware of the real significance and meaning of such a mission in the eyes of the Ch'ing Court. The Chinese Emperor and the Nepalese government had different views regarding the 1789 Nepalese mission to China. To the Chinese Emperor, the 1789 mission was a sign of Nepalese submission in the face of his army sent by him. This made it appear to the Chinese Emperor that the Nepalese were defeated. Here, it is important to recollect the story of Lord Macartney's mission to Peking in 1792-93, during which he carried with him, as a matter of courtesy, a large number of presents from King George III as a sign of England's goodwill towards the Emperor of China. In the Imperial decree of 4 February 1796, Emperor Ch'ien Lung, acknowledging the gift of the English King disclaimed any regard for the English "tribute", though valuing "the humble spirit which offers it". While addressing King George III of England, Ch'ing Emperor Ch'ien Lung used the following expressions: "Apparently you are unaware of this fact, so We do hereby inform you thereof while commanding Your humble loyalty to our Celestial Dynasty. We now present you with further gifts and command you to display continued energy and dutiful loyalty so as to deserve Our perpetual favour"[15]. Here it can be argued that if Nepal could be treated as a tributary to China on the basis of the Chinese decree, England must also be treated as a tributary of China, which cannot be accepted as fact. Therefore, it can be concluded that one must not attach too much importance to the Patent issued by the Chinese Emperor.

---

14 Leo E, Rose, *Nepal: Strategy For Survival*, Berkeley: University of California Press, 1971, p. 44.

15 Despatches from Her Britannic Majesty's Minister at Peking, 7 March 1911 and J.N. Jordan to Viceroy of India, 7 March 1911, Foreign Sec. E, July 1911, No. 264, NAI.

Here it should be pointed out that the Nepalese government, on the other hand, sent the 1789 mission to Peking to receive greater honours for their King. Wei-Yuan has also stated that the Chinese Commander actually persuaded the Gorkha Chieftain to bring tribute, in order to be appointed Prince of the country. While blaming the Chinese Commanders for all the misunderstanding and deceit, Wei-Yuan also commented that although not even a single pie was provided during the war, Pa-Chung produced a budget in which a million was spent on the soldiers' rations[16]. In this way, Pa-chung is said to have deceived the Ch'ing Court.

Significantly enough, it is still not clear as to why the Nepalese government, upon receipt of the Patent of 5 March, 1790, which conferred the Chinese titles to King Ran Bahadur Shah and Regent Bahadur Shah, did not bother to find out the exact meaning of the Chinese titles. Similarly, it is not known whether or not the Nepalese government was aware of the fact that the Chinese title really implied, at least from the Chinese perspective, Chinese suzerainty over Nepal. It can be assumed that the Nepalese rulers seemed to have been greatly pleased at the bestowal of the Chinese titles upon them by the Chinese Emperor, thinking those titles to be of higher status, or that the Nepalese rulers, after finding out the Chinese perception regarding the titles, remained silent as if they were not aware of the meaning and significance of the Chinese titles. Whatever the case may be, it should be pointed out that little significance can be attributed to the Chinese document (Patent) concerning the feudatory status of Nepal, given that all of the Ch'ing (Chinese) Empire's relations were of necessity conducted in terms of tributary relationships. Furthermore, it can be also argued that

---

16 Landon, f.n. no. 13, pp. 275-282.

the offering of titles by one sovereign to another sovereign does not imply that the receipient of the title is under the sovereignty of the bestower of the title. Finally, in the context of the Chinese title which indicated that the Nepalese King was a feudatory of the Chinese Emperor, here it should be mentioned that the British government had also conferred the title of Honorary Colonel to Nepalese Prime Minister Chandra Shamsher. Was then Chandra Shamsher, the Prime Minister of an independent country, only a Colonel in the British army ?

Here it will be worthwhile to mention that upon receipt of the Chinese Patent of 5 March, 1790, the Nepalese King appears to have sent through the Chinese *Amban* in Tibet a petition, expressing his thanks and requesting to be allowed to send people to Tibet to study the Chinese written language in order to be able to compose petitions more conveniently[17].

In this way, it can be stated that the Chinese Patent of 5 March, 1790 has its own importance in the annals of Nepal-China relations, for it was through this very Patent that Ran Bahadur Shah became the first Nepalese King to receive the Chinese title of "Ertini Wang", and this very Chinese title was used by Nepalese Kings from Girvanyuddha Vikram to Prithvi Bir Vikram in reference to themselves while addressing the Chinese Court. Furthermore, it also clearly and certainly indicates that the Nepalese mission of 1789 was the first one to go to China in modern times, but that was definitely not a five-yearly mission, for the Chinese Patent did not mention anything about the five-yearly mission. Thus it can be said that the Chinese Patent of 1790 started a new phase in Nepal-China relations.

17 J.N. Jordan to Govt. of India, 7 March 1911, Foreign Sec. E, July 1911, No. 264, NAI.

Appendix A*

Patent of 5th March 1790

The Mandate of His Majesty the Emperor, on whom by the dispensation of Heaven has devolved the succession to the Throne.

A special decree to you Ranabahadur, King of Nepal ! Your people live to the south of Tibet, and harmonious relations have hitherto prevailed between the Tibetans and yourselves. Trade has regularly been carried on between north and south, but unexpectedly We learn that last year you, Nepalese, suddenly made war on Tibet. Whereupon, We commanded Our Resident at Lhasa to take the necessary measures, and your General was punished and driven back. Afterwards, Our General Yang Yao was despatched with full powers, and We are now in receipt of his memorial which reports that the Tibetan Kablon Sonomvangehel had increased the rates of private duties on merchandise, and that he and his colleagues have unjustly resorted to acts of deceit and treachery against you, Nepalese. You, feeling unable to endure these extortions, accordingly acted as you did. Such is the memorial that Our imperial commissioner has submitted to Us. We have duly perused it together with your memorial accompanying the presentation of tribute.

Furthermore, We are apprised of Sonomvangehel's wilful hindrances and deceitful behaviour towards Our Resident in Lhasa. We have noted the terms of your memorial wherein

* Source: Foreign Secret E, July 1911, No. 264, National Archives of India(NAI), New Delhi. (Translated by E. Backhouse, Peking, 23rd February 1911).

you plead your innocence, and state that you were truly unable to put up with these exactions, which were the sole cause of your entering on hostilities. You acknowledge your error in stirring up trouble. Meantime, as Sonomvangehel has already died of disease, his case need not be further considered, but his son holding rank of a Daidji is hereby excluded from the succession and is banished to a malarious region 3,000 li away.

We have commanded the two Residents in Tibet to settle the business in which you were deceived as best they can and to see to it that the existing abuses are remedied. We are informed that you have advanced large bodies of troops over the frontier: these are to be withdrawn. Henceforward, when you despatch tribute mission and memorials to China, the various Tartar Generals and other provincial authorities are to secure proper escort for your mission along the road and to see to it that there be no delays. As to your private merchandise. We in Our Imperial condescension hereby grant you similar privileges as a special favour. We pardon you your rash action in entering upon hostilities. Ranabahadur ! show sincerity of heart ! Rule over your State, making honest purpose your chief guide, and as King of Nepal perform duly the service appointed by Us. Your tribute mission has duly reached Our capital and We have perused your memorial and examined your tribute. When the mission was introduced at Court, We conferred upon its members a special imperial banquet in token of Our high favour.

Ranabahadur, Prince of the Law, We hereby confer upon you the jewelled red button as bestowed upon princes, a court robe, four badges embroidered with dragons, four official coats of demi length, a necklace of 108 beads of amber, a girdle, purse and various fittings to match. On your son We confer the brevet rank of a duke, the ordinary coral first class button, a silken robe, a coat of demi length, a necklace of 108 beads of coral, a girdle, purse and appendages. On your senior minister

Harinbahadur Sahib (?) We confer the blue button and coat and robes corresponding to this rank.

In token of your desire to be included among the tributaries of Our dynasties, you Ranabahadur, your son and your respective ministers have sent to Us as tribute 4 complete rolls of Nepalese embroidered stuffs, 4 silver tea samovars weighing 50 ounces a piece and silver wine beakers of same weight, a pair of cloisonne incense burners and a pair of carved tea-cups. These We have duly examined and deign to accept. On the head of your tribute mission Harisahib We confer the fouth (fourth) blue button, a sable robe, a fur made up of breasts of white fox, a coat embroidered with dragons, a necklace, girdle and appurtenances to match. To each of the ten servants in his retinue We confer a sixth class white button, a peacock's feather, a snuff bottle, three rolls of silk, a tinder box, and five sacrificial bowls. On the second member of the mission We confer the foloth button, a sable robe, a coat embroidered with dragons, appurtenances to match, while We confer a sixth class white button, a peacock's feather, ten boxes of tea, three rolls of silk, and a snuff bottle on each member of his suite. We are the supreme lord of all under Heaven and show the same generous condescension to all. Our imperial protection is no respecter of persons and knows no boundaries. Even the humblest of Our subjects is entitled to the same measure of Our enfolding affection.

Out of Our love for you, We have shown to you exceptional condescension and in return you must display full reverence and respect for the law and maintain its ordinances. Such is the most important charge which We now make to you, Ranabahadur ! In Our good pleasure We have specially announced unto you this important imperial mandate. In future, do you obey Our orders to maintain peaceful relations with the Dalai and Panshen Erdini Lamas, and observe the existing regulations. Your people are to observe harmonious relations with the Tibetans, and you are each of you to carry on your trade in a spirit of mutual forbearance and justice. What has it profited you by entering upon hostilities ?

That Heaven may bless you, Our feudatory, with every happiness is indeed Our most earnest prayer !

A Special decree.

Ch'ien Lung, 55th year, 1st moon, 20th day.

Appendix B*

काजि हरि साहि वलभद्र षवासहरु मामुली सौगाद लि चीन जादाको लेषि आयाको.....

नेपाल र भोटको वेपारमा झगडा परी ताहावाट लुटी जवरजस्ती गऱ्यौ भनी सुन्दा लडाई गर्ना निमित ठूलो फौज पठायाको हो . भोटका मंत्री सोनाँ वांग्यालले थिचो गर्न लाग्दा सहन नसकी भोटहरु वस्ने अम्वाद्वारा अर्जि र सौगाद पठायाको निज सोनाँ वांग्यालले अंवासंग मिली जालसाज गर्दा यहा पुग्न नपायाको स्मेत जाहेर भयो यस्मा तिमीहरुको दोष रहेन छ निज अंवाहरुको वदला गरि दिन्यूं ठूलो दर्जाका हरि साहि र पाला वहादुर दोभासेहरु पठाई अर्जि सौगाद पठाउदा खुषि भै तिमिलाई अर्ति निवाङको दर्जा माणिकको गजुर टोपी र अरु चीजवीज स्मेत वक्सौं तिम्रा काका वहादुरलाई चौतरिया दर्जा मुगाको गजुर टोपी र अरु चीजवीज स्मेत वक्सौं भोटको रैती दुनीञा संग मिलाप गरी रहनु झगडा नगर्नु भंन्या छयालुं ५५ साल १ मैन्हा को श्री ५ माहाराजधिराज रण वहादुर साहका हजुरमा श्री ५ चीन वादशाहवाट आयाको प्रमाना १

(In this *Parwana* to King Ran Bahadur Shah, Chinese Emperor Ch'ien Lung has bestowed the Chinese titles to King Ran Bahadur Shah and Regent Bahadur Shah along with mentioning his pleasure at the sending of the Nepalese mission to China under the leadership of Hari Shahi).

***

---

* Source: Ministry of Foreign Affairs, Kathmandu, Poka No. Pa 64.

The Patent of 5 July 1870 and China's Claims of Suzerainty over Nepal*

Following the Nepal-Tibet war of 1788-1789, China's Ch'ing Emperor Ch'ien Lung had initiated direct relations with Nepal by bestowing upon Nepalese King Ran Bahadur Shah and Regent Bahadur Shah the Chinese titles of "Ertini Wang" and "Kung" (Ghung) respectively through the Patent of 5 March, 1790[1]. Since then the Chinese government had applied it indiscriminately with "Wang" to all the successive Kings of Nepal up to King Prithvi Bir Bikram Shah. Interestingly enough, though not formally decorated with this Chinese title, the Nepalese Kings from Girban Yuddha Bikram to Prithvi Bir Bikram used the term "Wang" for themselves while addressing to the Ch'ing court. As for the decoration of Nepalese Prime Ministers with Chinese titles, the case was somewhat quite different. It was at the request of the Nepalese King Rajendra Bikram Shah, Nepalese *Mukhtiyar* (Chief Minister) Bhimsen Thapa had received a Chinese title[2]. Likewise at the request of

---

* Unpublished Paper.

1 Patent of 5 March, 1790, J.N. Jordan to Viceroy of India, 7 March, 1911, Foreign Secret E, July 1911, No. 264, National Archives of India(NAI), New Delhi. Emperor Ch'ien Lung seemed to have conferred those Chinese titles hoping that Nepal would not be agressive towards Tibet in the future.

2 Shree Panch to *Ambans*, 1879 B.S. Poush Sudi 4 Roj 3 (December, 1822), Ministry of Foreign Affairs(MFA), Kathmandu, Unnumbered Poka. But Uprety has stated that King Ran Bahadur Shah had requested for the Ch'ing court to grant a Chinese title to Bhimsen Thapa. See Prem Uprety, "Honors, Medals and Honorific Titles: An

King Surendra Bikram Shah, Prime Minister Jang Bahadur Rana received the new Chinese title "Thong-Lin-Pimma-Kokang-Wang-Syan" through the Chinese Patent of 5 July 1870[3]. Till now, the Chinese Patent of 5 July 1870 conferring the Chinese title upon Jang Bahadur has not yet been properly discussed by anyone. In view of this, the main objective of this paper is to discuss the Chinese Patent of 5 July 1870 conferring the Chinese title upon Jang Bahadur by Emperor T'ung Chih. Besides that, China's claim of suzerainty over Nepal on the basis of the conferment of the said Chinese titles upon Rana Prime Minister Jang Bahadur Rana and his successors would be also dealt with.

Here it should be mentioned that due to her preoccupation in the Taiping rebellion, China could not militarily intervene in the Nepal-Tibet War of 1855-1856, thus indicating the declining of Chinese influence over Tibet. Furthermore her defeat in the second Anglo-Chinese War of 1856-1860 had also given her a bad image in the Himalayan area as well. As a result, China was in great need of regaining her former position in Tibet. With this view in mind, she decided to increase her contacts with Nepal. Two factors had made China a little uneasy. First, Nepal's role as an ally of British India during the Indian Mutiny of 1857 and secondly, Jang Bahadur's having received the title of "Knights Grand Cross of the Order of the Bath" in 1859 from the British government. Nepal's closer link with British India was potentially harmful to Chinese interests in Tibet; for a British-Nepalese combination to realize their interests in Tibet was a bogey which haunted the Ch'ing authorities in Tibet. Under such circumstance, China wanted to keep Nepal in good humour so that the latter would remain unopposed to Chinese interests in Tibet at the time of the decline of the Ch'ing dynasty's power. Therefore, according to

---

Understanding into the Nepali Historical Past", *Tribhuvan University Journal*, Vol. XVIII, June 1995, p. 5.

3 See Appendix

Chinese sources, the Ch'ing Emperor Hsien Feng in 1857-1858 was reported to have given presents and buttons of rank to Jang Bahadur and King Surendra Bikram Shah[4]. But according to British records, the Ch'ing Emperor sent six *Khilluts* (Apparel of honour) to King Surendra Bikram Shah, Prime Minister Jang Bahadur and to his four brothers, Generals Krishna Bahadur, Ranaudip Singh, Jagat Shamsher and Dhir Shamsher. The *Khilluts* consisted of silk, furs, agati cups amounting in value to about twelve thousand rupees. These *Khilluts* were sent to the Nepalese court by Emperor Hsien Feng" as tokens of his satisfaction at the successful termination of the war with Thibet"[5]. Besides that, even in 1860, through the Chinese officials at Lhasa, the Ch'ing Emperor Hsien Feng had asked Jang Bahadur to furnish an account of his services to the British in the Indian Mutiny of 1857 and the distinctions and rewards conferred upon him by Queen Victoria, for the Ch'ing Emperor also intended to bestow some equally high honour on Jang Bahadur[6]. It seemed that China considered it advantageous to develop closer relations with Nepal as one method of protecting its interests in Tibet from the independent-minded Tibetans and from the British. The Chinese sources state that the Ch'ing Emperor wanted the resumption of the Nepalese quinquennial missions, which the Taiping disturbances had interrupted. It was after the receipt of overtures from the Chinese *Amban* (Resident) at Lhasa that Jang Bahadur sent a mission to China in 1866[7], after the lapse of fourteen years. Here it should be also mentioned that in order to strengthen the Rana regime by increasing his own prestige and to safeguard Nepal's rights and privileges in Tibet obtained by the 1856 treaty, Jang Bahadur

---

4 E. H. Parker, "Nepaul and China", *The Imperial and Asiatic Quarterly Review and Oriental and Colonial Record*, Vol. VII, 1899, p. 81.

5 Resident in Nepal to Secretary, Govt. of India, 4 August, 1858, Foreign Dept. Sec., 27 August 1858, No. 96, NAI.

6 R.C. Lawrence to Govt. of India, 22 May 1871, Foreign Dept. Polt. A, July 1871, No. 100, NAI.

7 Ramsay to Secretary, Govt. of India, 9 June 1866, Foreign Dept. Polt. A, June 1866, No. 163, NAI.

too was eager to maintain good relations with China. Therefore, in May 1870 a Chinese Ambassador, *Taleh* (Tale) Kazi, visited Kathmandu and had talks with Jang Bahadur[8]. In this way, contacts between Nepal and China increased considerably after the Nepal-Tibet treaty of 1856. It was mainly guided by her self interest in maintaining her *status quo* position in Tibet that China followed the policy of keeping Nepal in good humour. As a result, Ch'ing Emperor T'ung Chih conferred a new Chinese title upon Jang Bahadur, the powerful Rana Prime Minister of Nepal.

When Jang Bahadur managed to wield full power over the state and government under the title of *Maharaja,* he wanted further glorification through the conferring of higher Chinese titles upon him from the Chinese Emperor as well. In fact he considered *Mukhtiyar* Bhimsen Thapa's Chinese title to be an inferior degree. In order to appease the Ch'ing Emperor, he dispatched the Nepalese mission to Peking in August 1866, and in May 1867, through King Surendra, requested for the Ch'ing Emperor to grant him a higher Chinese title. After much persuasion, Jang Bahadur succeeded in obtaining a new, high sounding Chinese title, "Thong-Lin-Pimma-Kokang-Wang-Syan" from Emperor T'ung Chih. Jang Bahadur's eagerness to obtain the Chinese title seemed to have been influenced by the following factors. Firstly, by receiving the high-sounding Chinese title from the Ch'ing Emperor, he wanted to present himself in the eyes of the Nepalese people as having being honoured by the Emperor of China, thus managing to receive glorification of his vanity. By receiving the Chinese title, he hoped to strengthen his position by receiving the stamp of approval from a ruler whose name carried great prestige. Thus the Chinese title certainly helped Jang Bahadur to boost his image in the eyes of the Nepalese people. Secondly, in order to safeguard Nepal's greater commercial interests in Tibet as well as to implement the clauses of the 1856 Nepal-Tibet treaty, Jang

8 Pudma Jang Bahadur Rana, *Life of Maharaja Sir Jung Bahadur*, Kathmandu: Ratna Pustak Bhandar, Reprint, 1980, p. 281.

Bahadur indeed needed the persistent goodwill of the Ch'ing Emperor. He seemed to have felt that by obtaining a higher Chinese title, a sign of 'favour' of the Chinese Emperor, the Nepalese position in Tibet would not be disregarded. Thus, in order to protect Nepal's extremely important commercial interests in Tibet, Jang Bahadur wanted to show 'a great allegiance' to the Ch'ing Emperor. With that in mind, King Surendra Bikram Shah was even reported to have written letters to the Ch'ing Emperor requesting 'some favour' for Jang Bahadur. Thirdly, Jang Bahadur also wanted to obtain the Chinese title in order to impress the British with Nepal's closer relations with China. In this way, by maintaining good relations with China, Jang Bahadur hoped to balance Nepal's relations with British India. Jang Bahadur too favoured King Prithvi Narayan Shah's counsel of maintaining balanced relations with China as well as with British India in order to safeguard Nepal's sovereignty and independence in the hey-days of the Great Chinese Empire and the expansion of the British Empire. Regarding the date of the conferring of the Chinese title upon Jang Bahadur, there is no unanimous opinion among the writers. Wright has mentioned that Jang Bahadur received the Chinese title in 1871[9], as have Manandhar and Mojumdar[10]. Rose has given the date as 19 April, 1871[11], whereas Jang Bahadur's son and biographer Pudma Jung gives the date as 19 April, 1872[12]. This date has also been mentioned by Landon and Purushottam Shamsher[13]. Strangely enough, Levi stated that Jang Bahadur

---

9 Daniel Wright (ed.), *History of Nepal*, Translated from *Parbatiya*, Second Edition, Calcutta: Susil Gupta (India) Private Ltd., Reprint, 1958, p. 176.

10 Tri Ratna Manandhar, Nepal: *The Years of Trouble (1877-85)*, Kathmandu: Purna Devi Manandhar, 1986, p. 139 and Kanchanmoy Mojumdar, *Political Relations between India and Nepal (1877-1923)*, New Delhi: Munshiram Manoharlal Publishers Pvt. Ltd., 1973, p. 82.

11 Leo E. Rose, *Nepal: Strategy For Survival*, Berkeley: University of California Press, 1971, p. 136.

12 Pudma Jung, f.n. no. 8, pp. 284-285.

13 Perceval Landon, *Nepal*, Vol. I, Kathmandu: Ratna Pustak Bhandar, Reprint, 1987, p. 153 and Purushottam Shamsher JBR, *Sri Tin Haruko*

received the Chinese title in 1858[14], but going through the Indian archival documents, it becomes quite evident that Emperor T'ung Chih had already conferred the Chinese title on 5 July 1870[15] and that the formal presentation ceremony of the Chinese title to Jang Bahadur took place around April 1871[16]. For the purpose of conferring the new title of distinction on Jang Bahadur, Emperor T'ung Chih dispatched a special Chinese envoy to Kathmandu[17]. In April 1871[18], during a function at which the Nepalese monarch and the British Resident were also present, Jang Bahadur received the Chinese title of "Thong-Lin-Pimma-Kokang-Wang-Syan" (Thong-Ling-Pimma-Kokang-Wang - Shang) accompanied by a Chinese robe of honour of double eyed peacock feathers and a sable coat from the Chinese envoy. Dances and music were performed in Kathmandu to celebrate the happy occasion. After staying a few days in the Nepalese capital, the Chinese envoy left Kathmandu for Peking[19]. In connection with the Chinese title, one writer has stated that the Chinese Emperor had sent the Chinese title to Jang Bahadur through the 1870 Nepalese mission to China[20].

Tathya Brittanta, (Factual Descriptions of Sri Tins), Banaras: Parambir Shamsher J.B.R, 2047 B.S., p. 132.

14 Sylvain Levi, "Nepal" translated into English, published in *Ancient Nepal,* Journal of Department of Archaeology, Kathmandu, No. 28, July 1974, p. 46.

15 See Appendix.

16 See Abstract Translation of a *Yaddasht* (Memorandum) from *Maharaja* Jang Bahadur to R.C. Lawrence, 5 April 1871, Foreign Dept. Polt A, July 1871, No. 101, NAI.

17 R.C. Lawrence to Secretary, Govt. of India, 22 May 1871, Foreign Dept. Polt. A, July 1871, No. 100, NAI.

18 Abstract translation of a *Yaddasht* from *Maharaja* Jang Bahadur to R.C. Lawrence, 5 April 1871, Foreign Dept. Polt. A, July 1871, No. 101, NAI.

19 "Nepal Desh Ko Itihas" (History of Nepal), A Manuscript in the National Archives of Nepal, Kathmandu, Published in *Ancient Nepal,* No. 27, April 1974, p. 13 and Pudma Jung, f.n. no. 8, p. 281.

20 Ramesh Dhungel, "Aitihasik Chinia Padak--Thong Lin Pimma Kokang Wang Syan" (Historical Chinese Title--Thong Lin Pimma Kokang

This is far from truth. Firstly, the Indian archival documents clearly indicate that the Chinese Emperor had dispatched an envoy especially for the purpose of conferring the Chinese title upon Jang Bahadur. The practice of dispatching Chinese envoys especially for the purpose of conferring Chinese titles upon the successive Rana Prime Ministers of Nepal was continued by the Ch'ing Emperors. Secondly, Jang Bahadur sent the Nepalese mission to China not in 1870 but in 1866, which was not even allowed to visit Peking allegedly because of a Muslim rebellion in western China. Thirdly, the 1866 Nepalese mission had returned to the Nepalese capital by 1869. Another point which must be mentioned was that perhaps consequent to the bestowal of the Chinese title through the Patent of 5 July 1870, Prime Minister Jang Bahadur was decorated with the title of "Knight Grand Commander of the Most Exalted Order of the Star of India" by British Queen Victoria in May 1873[21].

Jang Bahadur seemed to have felt very proud of this new high-sounding Chinese title of "Thong-Lin-Pimma-Kokang-Wang-Syan" which he translated as "the highly honoured (the most noble) Commander and Controller of Military and Political Affairs, the Augmenter and Instructor (disciplinarian) of the Army, the Aggrandizer of the Country, the Satisfier of the Low and High by increasing the prosperity and revenue of the Country, the Great Inheritor of Fidelity and Faithfulness to the Salt"[22]. Regarding this Chinese title, writers have given different meanings. As translated by Pudma Jung, the Chinese title meant "Leader of the Army, the Most Brave in every Enterprise, Perfect in Everything, Master of the Brave People, Mighty Maharaja"[23]. Likewise, Wright has given the meaning of the Chinese title as "Leader of the army, the most brave in every

Wang Syan), *Smarika* (Souvenir), No. 4-5, Kathmandu: Nepal-China Friendship Association, 2043 B.S., pp. 34-35.

21 Pudma Jung, f.n. no. 8, p. 314.

22 R.C. Lawrence to Secretary, Govt. of India, 22 May 1871, Foreign Dept. Polt. A, July 1871, No. 100, N.A.I.

23 Pudma Jung, f.n. no. 8 , p. 285.

enterprise, perfect in everything, master of the army, Maharaj"[24]. Landon has mentioned the meaning of the Chinese title as "Truly Valiant Prince, Commander-in-Chief of the army"[25]. Levi has given the meaning of the Chinese title as "General-in-Chief of the army, Prince really brave (truly brave prince) and Prime Minister"[26]. According to a Chinese-English Dictionary, compiled by Peking Foreign Language Institute, English Department, the meaning of the aforementioned Chinese title appears as "Leading Soldier and Cavalry (Army) together determined and daring Maharaja Prime Minister."[27] In 1910 when the Chinese government claimed her suzerainty over Nepal on the bases of the decoration of Nepalese Prime Ministers with the Chinese title of "Thong-Lin-Pimma-Kokang-Wang-Syan", according to one Nepalese document Prime Minister Chandra Shamsher tried to obtain the meaning of the said Chinese title through the Nepalese *Vakil* (envoy) at Lhasa. Afterwards, the Nepalese *Vakil* sent to Premier Chandra Shamsher the four different meanings of the said Chinese title provided by the Chinese-Nepalese interpreters. While examining the four different meanings of the Chinese title, it becomes evident that a higher Chinese title was bestowed upon *Raja-Maharaja* (rulers and Prime Ministers) and on the Military and Civilian Chief of

---

24 Wright, f.n. no. 9, p. 176.

25 Landon, f.n. no. 13, pp. 246-247.

26 Levi, f.n. no. 14, p. 46. See also, Historical Note on Relations between Nepal and China by F.A. Hirtzel, 4 November 1910, Foreign Sec. E, July 1911, No. 250, NAI.

27
Tung-	Together
Ling-	To lead (to lead troops into battle)
Ping-	Soldier (Land soldier)
Ma-	Horse
Kuo-	Resolute, determined (fruitful)
Kan-	Bold, courageous, daring
Wang-	King, Monarch (Maharaja)
Hsien-	Rank, Title (Prime Minister)

Peking Foreign Language Institute (Comp.), A Chinese-English Dictionary, Peking: Commercial Publication House, 1978.

a state[28]. Likewise, the Chinese *Amban* at Lhasa was reported to have translated the Chinese title as "Being Valorous, able, bravely to meet any emergency, accompanied by or at the head of the whole army, accomplished in everything, head or master of the military, *Wang* Raja"[29]. But the Nepalese official translation describes the Chinese title as the "Commander-in-Chief of both army and cavalry and the Prime Minister of the Gorkha King"[30].

Interestingly enough, one writer has stated that Chandra Shamsher happened to be the first Nepalese Prime Minister to receive the Chinese title "Thong-Lin-Pimma-Kokang-Wang-Syan", in 1959 B.S. (1902 A.D.)[31]. But this is quite untrue, for it is a historical fact that Jang Bahadur was the first Nepalese Prime Minister to be conferred with that Chinese title. Besides him, Rana Ministers Ranaudip Singh[32], Bir Shamsher[33] and

---

28 For the details of the four different meanings of the Chinese title, See Dhungel, f.n. no. 20, p. 35 and Tirtha Prasad Mishra, "Sri Tin Maharaja Chandra Shamsher Ra Chinia Samman" (Prime Minister Chandra Shamsher and Chinese Honour), *Ancient Nepal,* Nos. 98-99, February-May 1987, pp. 11-12.

29 Chandra Shamsher to J. Manners Smith, 29 November 1910, Foreign Sec. E, January 1911, No. 181, NAI.

30 MFA, E1, Poka 15.

31 Kamalmani Dixit, "Batha Matrai Hun Ki ?" (Was Clever only ?), *Nepali,* Nepali Quarterly, No. 98, Magh 2040 B.S., p. 38. Dixit has stated that Chandra Shamsher had received the Chinese title in 1959 B.S. (1902 A.D.), But the Nepalese and Indian archival documents clearly point out that Chandra Shamsher received the Chinese title on 17 April 1904 (6 Baisakh, 1961 B.S.). See, Ravenshaw to Foreign Dept., 20 April 1904, Foreign Sec. E, September 1904, No. 88, NAI. For the detailed Nepalese account of conferring the Chinese title on Premier Chandra Shamsher, See, Mishra, f.n. no. 28, pp. 4-13.

32 A Special Chinese envoy arrived at Kathmandu and formally conferred the Chinese title upon Prime Minister Ranaudip Singh in January 1878. See, Henvey to Aitchison, 18 January 1878, Foreign Dept. Polt. A, February 1878, No. 178, NAI.

33 A Chinese envoy came to Kathmandu in August 1889 and decorated Prime Minister Bir Shamsher with the Chinese title, See "Nepal Desh Ko Itihas" (History of Nepal), *Ancient Nepal,* No. 27, April 1974, p. 31.

Chandra Shamsher were also decorated with the same Chinese title. As regards Rana Prime Minister Dev Shamsher, one Nepalese document clearly indicates that he was notified of the Ch'ing Emperor's granting of the same Chinese title to him[34], but before the ceremony could be held for the formal presentation of the Chinese title, Prime Minister Dev Shamsher was deposed by Chandra Shamsher in a bloodless coup in June 1901. In this way, Dev Shamsher, who could remain Prime Minister for only one hundred and four days, could not be formally decorated with the Chinese title. Thus, considering the above discussion, it becomes quite evident that Chandra Shamsher happened to be not the first, but the last Nepalese Prime Minister to receive that Chinese title.

Upon examining the Patent of 5 July 1870[35], one will become aware of the following points. Firstly, Ch'ing Emperor T'ung Chih had mentioned the restoration of peace and the granting of high rewards to all state officials including the Ch'ing's feudatories at the suppression of the rebellions (the Taiping rebellion lasted from 1850 to 1864, and the Nien rebellion lasted from 1853 to 1868 and nearly toppled the Ch'ing dynasty itself). Secondly, Nepalese Premier Jang Bahadur seemed to have sent a message of congratulations to the Ch'ing Emperor concerning the suppression of the rebellions. Following this, the Emperor granted a special rank to Jang Bahadur. The Emperor had stated that he had then received a request for additional honours to be accorded to Jang Bahadur. He further added that in recognition of Jang Bahadur's complete sincerity towards the Emperor, he, thereby, conferred upon Jang Bahadur "the Brevet Rank of General of a Banner". Besides that, Emperor T'ung Chih included in special patent bestowed on Jang Bahadur, the honorific appellation of "Sincere". Thirdly,

---

34 Chinese *Amban* to King Prithvi Bir Bikram, Kwang Sui 27th year 6th month 11th day, National Archives of Nepal, Kathmandu, Poka No. 2, Letter No. 141.

35 See Appendix.

while conferring the aforementioned rank and the special Patent, Emperor T'ung Chih gave instructions for Jang Bahadur to continue to exert himself with his whole strength. The Emperor had also clearly stated that he, as a special favour, had conferred upon Jang Bahadur special patents and had instructed the Nepalese Prime Minister to do his utmost as ruler of the country and to ensure the maintenance of peace and freedom from internal disturbances. Fourthly, the Ch'ing Emperor had hinted his commendation at the rendering of Jang Bahadur's past services, perhaps indicating Jang Bahadur's offering help to the Ch'ing throne by providing ten thousand Nepalese soldiers to crush the Taiping rebellion[36]. Fifthly, it also clearly indicates that whatever meaning may have been attached to the Chinese title "Thong-Lin-Pimma-Kokang-Wang-Syan" conferred upon Nepalese Prime Ministers, the said Chinese title did denote the feudatory status of the receipients.

Interestingly enough, China claimed her suzerainty over Nepal in 1910. One of the bases of the Chinese claim was the bestowal of the Chinese title of 'Thong-Lin-Pimma-Kokang-Wang-Syan" upon the Rana Prime Ministers of Nepal. In November 1910, while talking to the British Resident J.Manners Smith, Nepalese Prime Minister Chandra Shamsher stated that he could not say whether the Chinese title of "Thong-Lin-Pimma-Kokang-Wang-Syan" which was bestowed on the ruling Prime Ministers of Nepal implied any acceptance of Chinese suzerainty on the part of Nepal. The Nepalese Prime Minister suggested to the British Resident that that point could be best ascertained by contacting the British Minister at Peking, where

36 Jnanmani Nepal, "Jang Bahadur Ko Bidesh Niti Ra Sambat 1904 Ko Pechin Jane Pratinidhi Mandal" (Jang Bahadur's Foreign Policy and Mission to Pechin of 1904 B.S.), *Contributions to Nepalese Studies*, Vol. VIII, No. 2 (June 1981), p. 181. Here it should be noted that the Nepalese offer was declined by the Ch'ing court on the grounds of the great distance between Nepal and China and the Chinese tradition of not receiving aid from outside countries.

the exact meaning of the Chinese title could be known[37]. However, the British Minister at Peking stated that he was unable to identify the full titles conferred on the Nepalese Prime Ministers and asked to be furnished with the full titles given to the Prime Ministers of Nepal in Chinese characters[38]. Accordingly, Chandra Shamsher sent the original letter from Empeor T'ung Chih written on the occasion of the conferment of the title of "Thong-Lin-Pimma-Kokang-Wang-Syan" on Prime Minister Jang Bahadur in 1870. He also added that the then *Amban* at Lhasa, in his letter written in *Parbatiya* (Nepali) language intimating the bestowal of the title on Jang Bahadur (which title had since been received by every successive Prime Minister) explained the meaning of the title as well[39]. The Nepalese Prime Minister asked the British Minister at Peking to supply a literal translation in English of the Chinese portion in the letter referred to above, as well as to return the original at the same time. Upon the receipt of the original letter sent by the Nepalese Premier, the British Minister at Peking stated that Emperor T'ung Chih's letter was written in the Manchu and not in the Chinese language, and, this being the case, it would consequently be a matter of some difficulty to obtain an accurate and reliable translation[40]. In the meantime, he had also stated that the Nepalese Premier could be asked whether or not he would also like to receive translations of the Tibetan and Turkish portions of the letter referred to above. Finally, J.N. Jordan, the British Minister at Peking, sought the help of Edmund Backhouse, a British student of Oriental languages residing in the city of Peking, who translated the Manchu

---

37 J.Manners Smith to Govt. of India, 1 November-7 November 1910, Foreign Sec. E, January 1911, No. 166, NAI.

38 His Britannic Majesty's Minister, Peking to Viceroy of India, 24 November 1910, Foreign Sec. E, January 1911, No. 175, NAI.

39 For the Chinese *Amban's* translation of the Chinese title, See Chandra Shamsher to J.Manners Smith, 29 November 1910, Foreign Sec. E, January 1911, No. 181, NAI.

40 J.N. Jordan to Govt. of India, 4 February 1911, Foreign Sec. E, July 1911, No. 259, NAI.

portion of the Patent conferred by Ch'ing Emperor T'ung Chih on Prime Minister Jang Bahadur, and remarked that the translations be considered as substantially accurate. From Peking, on 7 March 1911, J.N. Jordan dispatched along with remarks, a translation of the Manchu portion of the Patent conferred by the Ch'ing Emperor on Jang Bahadur. While returning the original Patent by registered parcel post, J.N. Jordan remarked that the actual title conferred by the Ch'ing Emperor's Patent was such as would be bestowed on the ministers of feudatory states. He mentioned that the English rendering of the Manchu characters for the title conferred on Premier Jang Bahadur in 1870 was "Brevet Rank of General of a Banner" (i.e., the Highest Rank in the Manchu Military Organization) which did not entirely coincide with the Chinese *Amban's* Chinese transliteration of the characters used in the Tibetan portion of the Patent. Meanwhile, the British Minister had also remarked that the discrepancy suggested the possibility of the existence of other differences between the various portions (Manchu, Tibetan and Turkish) of those trilingual documents but that there was no doubt however, that the Manchu portion must in each case be considered to prevail. As such he suggested that it might be advisable to obtain English translations of the Tibetan and Turkish portions for the purpose of comparison[41]. It was reported that Chandra Shamsher was afraid that it would not be possible to make a reliable translation of the Tibetan version of the 1870 Patent in Nepal. Experiencing great difficulty in getting translations, the British government decided not to take the trouble to obtain translations of either the Tibetan or Turkish version of the said Patent. The British government regarded the text of the Patent to be of minor importance in view of the fact that the British government had by that time definitely told China that it would resist any attempt on China's part to impose authority on, or interfere with

41 Same to Same, 7 March 1911, Foreign Sec. E, July 1911, No. 264, NAI.

Nepal in any way[42]. The translation which the British Minister sent from Peking was not encouraging to the Nepalese government. Meanwhile, Chandra Shamsher denied that the Chinese titles to the Nepalese Prime Ministers in any way indicated Nepal's feudatory status *vis-a-vis* China[43].

Here it should be mentioned that, like Jang Bahadur, his successors too, became fond of Chinese titles. For this reason, the Nepalese Kings Surendra Bikram and Prithvi Bir Bikram were made to request for the Ch'ing Emperors to confer the Chinese title "Thong-Lin-Pimma-Kokang-Wang-Syan" upon Nepalese Prime Ministers Ranaudip Singh, Bir Shamsher, Dev Shamsher and Chandra Shamsher. Hence it became a custom for the Ch'ing government to send a Chinese mission or representative to Kathmandu to decorate the new Prime Minister of Nepal with that Chinese title and the robes connected with it. So afterwards it became some sort of a fashion or a status symbol for the Nepalese Rana Prime Ministers to obtain the above mentioned Chinese title with the aim of getting Chinese recognition of their rule. According to the Nepalese and Indian archival documents, the Chinese envoy was welcomed with marked distinction. A guard of honour with a band was sent two miles north of the capital to escort him in, and a grand *Darbar* (court) was held by the Prime Minister for his reception. A formal ceremony was held at the royal palace, where the Chinese envoy, in the presence of the Nepalese King and members of the nobility and the clergy, presented the Chinese title and robes to the Nepalese Prime Minister in the midst of a nineteen gun salute [44] The scene was made all the more

---

42 Resident in Nepal to Secretary, Govt. of India, 18 May 1911, Foreign Sec. E, July 1911, No. 264, NAI.

43 Chandra Shamsher to J. Manners Smith, 19 November 1910, Foreign Dept. Sec. E, January 1911, No. 178, NAI.

44 "Nepal Desh Ko Itihas" (History of Nepal), *Ancient Nepal*, No. 27, April 1974, p. 31 and Mishra, f.n. no. 28, pp. 7-9. See also, Henvey to Aitchison, 18 January 1878, Foreign Dept. Polt. A., February 1878, No. 178, NAI.

dramatic when the Nepalese Prime Minister bowed in a kneeling posture facing northeast expressing his extreme delight and gratitude to the Ch'ing Emperor. There also used to be rejoicing in the Nepalese capital to celebrate the happy occasion[45]. Prime Minister Jang Bahadur's successors' fondness for Chinese titles also seemed to have been motivated by the same factors as those of Jang Bahadur. Furthermore, as the legality of the accession to offices of some of them could be also questioned, the Rana Prime Ministers hoped to strengthen their positions through recognition by the Ch'ing throne. That is why there were several instances of persuasion through letters from the Nepalese Kings to the Ch'ing Emperors for the bestowal of Chinese titles and robes to the Nepalese Prime Ministers. One very interesting point regarding the Chinese title was that the Rana Prime Ministers were not acquainted with the real meaning and significance of the Chinese title, for they had regarded the Chinese title to be a very prestigious honour from the Ch'ing Emperor. It was, however, only in the first decade of the twentieth century that they became aware of the fact that the Chinese titles and robes, of which they were fond and proud, really implied at least from the Chinese perspective, Chinese suzerainty over Nepal. Therefore in 1910, China formally claimed her suzerainty over Nepal on the grounds of having conferred the Chinese titles upon Nepalese Prime Ministers as well. Interestingly enough, at that very time, Premier Chandra Shamsher was seeking 'some favour' in the form of another Chinese title and honour from the Ch'ing Emperor. So in 1910, once he came to know the Chinese grounds for the claim of suzerainty over Nepal, Chandra Shamsher instantly decided not to accept any sort of 'title' from the Ch'ing Emperor. On this basis it can be stated that the Rana Prime Ministers were not aware of the real meaning and significance of the Chinese title. Otherwise, they would have surely had second thoughts before receiving the Chinese title. It should be clearly pointed out that

45 Prem R.Uprety, *Nepal-Tibet Relations 1850-1930*, Kathmandu: Puga Nara, 1980, pp. 193-194.

despite all sorts of blame for their deeds during the entire Rana period, the Rana Prime Ministers were certainly quite sensitive about the question of Nepal's sovereignty and independence, for they did not compromise in Nepal's sovereignty and independence at all. They were nationalists *in toto;* it is a historical fact that with the help of the British, they not only repudiated the Chinese claim of suzerainty over Nepal by terminating the quinquennial mission system in 1911, but also skilfully managed to obtain the British government's recognition of Nepal's sovereignty and independence through the treaty of 1923.

Here it is also worthwhile to discuss China's perspective regarding the bestowing of Chinese titles upon the Prime Ministers of Nepal. With the gradual decline of her influence in Tibetan affairs following the Taiping rebellion and Nepal-Tibet war of 1855-1856, as well as Nepal's increasingly closer ties with British India, for her self interest in maintaining her *status quo* position in Tibet, China had tried to keep Nepal in good humour so that Nepal would continue to show her allegiance to the Ch'ing Emperor. For that reason, China started the system of conferring a new Chinese title upon the powerful Rana Prime Ministers of Nepal from the time of Jang Bahadur. In addition to that, through the system of conferring Chinese titles to the Nepalese Prime Ministers, China could not only glorify herself as a Great Empire but also claim Nepal as a vassal of China, which added the prestige to the Chinese Empire that the Chinese eagerly sought.

In the final analysis it can be concluded that the Chinese Patent of 5 July 1870 inaugurated the Ch'ing court's new system of conferring the Chinese title of "Thong-Lin-Pimma-Kokang-Wang-Syan" to Jang Bahadur and his successive Prime Ministers. The Rana Prime Ministers, on the other hand, seemed to have received the Chinese titles without knowing the real meaning and significance of the Chinese titles which denoted the feudatory status of the recipients. Regarding the Chinese claim of suzerainty over Nepal, it can be stated that the Rana Prime Ministers were not the *De Jure* but the *de facto* rulers of Nepal As such, it would not be reasonable to treat Nepal as feudatory state of China simply on the grounds of the decoration of the Nepalese Prime Ministers with the Chinese titles. Besides that, the real fact was that the Rana Prime Ministers and the Ch'ing Emperors had different perspectives regarding the Chinese titles. The Chinese titles and honours had only a formal value. It certainly satisfied China's ego but on the otherhand it added to the prestige of the Rana Prime Ministers of Nepal in the eyes of the British and Nepalese people, although the latter did not know the meaning of the title.

Appendix

Patent of 5th July 1870

The Mandate of His Majesty the Emperor, on whom has devolved by the dispensation of Heaven the heritage of the Throne.

Caring anxiously for the welfare of all Our Dominions and entertaining nought but feelings of Charity in Our heart, now that the rebellions against Our Throne have been defeated, We have indited decrees in celebration of the restoration of peace. To all Our officials, great and small, whether metropolitan or provincial, We have in Our Imperial clemency granted high rewards. For exceptional services We confer exceptional favours. To Our respective Ministries We have announced Our intention of bestowing the rewards provided for bv precedent. Therefore, it behoves Us to bestow special marks of merit on Our respective feudatories. Let this be recognised as a peculiar mark of Our favour in order that the sincerity of Our feelings may be made manifest !

Jang Bahadur, Chief Minister of Nepal ! We have perused your memorial of congratulation. To you Jang Bahadur special rank has been granted. We have now received the request that additional honours should be accorded to you. In all the region of Nepal, where We have given you the appointment, there exists complete sincerity towards Us. Therefore, We do hereby now confer upon you, Jang Bahadur, the Brevet Rank of General of a Banner, and in Special Patent bestow upon you the honorific appellation of "Sincere". You must continue to exert yourself with your whole strength: for services already rendered We accord to you our commendation.

Hadji (?) Jang Bahadur, since We in Our special favour do confer upon you these Special Patents, you must show your utmost endeavours as ruler of the country and must ensure the maintenance of peace and freedom from internal disturbances.

May Heaven bless your State with happiness and prosperity ! This is Our earnest hope ! A most important decree.

T'ung Chih, 9th year, 6th moon, 7th day.

***

Source: Foreign Dept. Sec. E, July 1911, No. 264, National Archives of India (NAI), New Delhi. (Translated by E. Backhouse, Peking, 22nd February 1911)

Kazi Bhairab Bahadur's Mission To China*

The system of sending Nepalese quinquennial missions to China had its origin in the peace agreement of September, 1792 between the Nepalese and Chinese officials following the ending of the Sino-Nepalese War of 1791-1792. From 1792 to 1906, Nepal sent altogether eighteen customary five-yearly missions to China. The mission of 1906, the eighteenth and the last Nepalese quinquennial mission to the Imperial Court of China, was led by *Kazi* Major Bhairab Bahadur Gadhatola Chhetri. So far multidimensional aspects of the mission are not retain. Hence an attempt is made here to do justice to them on the basis of the original unpublished documents preserved in the National Archives of India in New Delhi.

Leo E. Rose has referred to the leader of the 1906 Nepalese quinquennial mission to China as Bharat Bahadur[1]. The Indian Archival documents prove that it was *Kazi* Bhairab Bahadur Gadhatola Chhetri who led the Nepalese mission of 1906 to China[2]. The deputy-leader of the mission was *Sardar*

---

* Published in *Journal of Nepalese Studies*, Vol. I, No. 1 (March 1996), pp. 101-108 and *Rolamba*, Vol. 16, No. 2 (April-June 1996), pp. 12-18.

1 Leo E. Rose, *Nepal: Strategy For Survival*, Berkeley: University of California Press, 1971, p. 164, and Margaret W. Fisher and Leo E. Rose, *England, India, Nepal, Tibet, China, 1765-1958*, Berkeley: University of California, 1959, pp. 2-12.

2 J. Manners Smith to Secretary, Govt. of India, 17 August 1906, Foreign Department Sec. E, September 1906, No. 263, National Archives of India (NAI), New Delhi.

Kahar Singh Khadka[3]. *Kazi* Bhairab Bahadur Gadhatola was the son of Major Captain Mahavir Gadhatola Chhetri, a veteran of the Indian Mutiny, who had served as Nepal's *Vakil*(envoy) at Lhasa during the crucial period from 1882 to 1886[4]. Major Bhairab Bahadur was formerly Orderly Officer to the British Residency in Nepal for thirteen years. He had received the rank of *Kazi* for the purpose of the mission. A few days before his departure, the Nepalese Prime Minister Chandra Shamsher had sent Major Bhairab Bahadur to pay the British Resident in Nepal, Major J. Manners Smith, a formal call before leaving Kathmandu. During that call, Major Bhairab Bahadur had asked the British Resident to furnish him with a letter to the British representative in China to serve as an introduction on his arrival in Peking. The Nepalese quinquennial mission to Peking left Kathmandu on 10 August 1906[5]. It was well received by both the Chinese and Tibetan officials at the Nepal-Tibet border. As *Kazi* Bhairab Bahadur fell ill in Shigatse, he went to Gyantse, reaching there on 16 October 1906 to get medical help from the British. The other members of the mission went from Shigatse to Lhasa *via* the Rong valley. On 21 October 1906, Major Bhairab Bahadur called on Lieutenant F.M. Bailey, officiating British Trade Agent at Gyantse and expressed his gratitude for the British medical help which he had obtained there. He also told Lieutenant Bailey that he preferred to go by sea but Chinese government insisted on his coming by road follow like the earlier the Nepalese missions. He also stated that the costs incurred by the Chinese government would be more than the value of the presents he was carrying for the Chinese Emperor, which were worth about twenty thousand rupees.

---

3 Translation of a news-letter from *Kazi* Bhairab Bahadur, 15 February 1909, Foreign Department Sec. E, June 1909, No. 478, NAI.

4 J. N. Jordan to Edward Grey, 5 June 1908, Foreign Department Sec. E, October 1908, No. 709, NAI. The Crisis of 1883 placed both Nepal and Tibet in a war-like situation which ended only after a long negotiation in 1884.

5 J. Manners Smith to Secretary, Government of India, 17 August 1906, Foreign Department Sec. E, September 1906, No. 263, NAI.

Lieutenant Bailey had described *Kazi* Bhairab Bahadur an "intelligent" man who spoke English fluently and read all the books in English available to him[6]. The Nepalese *Kazi* left Gyantse for Lhasa on 23 October 1906. It seems that he had arrived in Lhasa by January, 1907, from whence he wrote a letter in English to the Nepalese Prime Minister regarding the details of his arrival at Lhasa along with a brief account of the journey. The Nepalese mission left Lhasa for Peking on 6 February 1907[7].

Upon his arrival at Bathang, *Kazi* Bhairab Bahadur met an American named Henry Endemenilt, who after staying in Japan for two years came to China, where he was a school teacher in Peking and Tientsin. The Nepalese envoy's meeting and conversation with this American gentleman was friendly. The American teacher gave the Nepalese envoy a letter of introduction to the American Minister at Peking. Besides that, he also informed the Nepalese envoy about the edict prohibiting the use of opium by the Chinese government servants and the public, and thus the diminishing consumption of opium. The Nepalese court had also sent opium with this mission to be sold in China[8]. The Nepalese envoy left Bathang on 21 May 1907 and reached Lithang on 27 May 1907. Through a letter dated 17 August 1907 from Tarchindeo, the Nepalese *Kazi* informed Premier Chandra Shamsher that the opium which he had brought with him for sale on government account had not yet been sold and he believed that the opium could not be sold on the open market due to the Chinese government's policy of closing the smoking dens and the gradual restriction of the use of opium among the people. He also stated that in the event that it was impossible to dispose of the opium stock by any means,

6 Diary of Lieutenant F.M. Bailey, Officiating Trade Agent at Gyantse, 20 October- 27 October 1906, Foreign Dept. Sec. E, July 1907, Nos. 304-305, NAI.

7 Translation of a letter from the Nepalese representative at Lhasa, 18 February 1907, Foreign Dept. Sec. E, June 1907, No. 88, NAI.

8 J. Manners Smith to Assistant Secretary, Govt. of India, 7 August 1907, Foreign Dept. Sec. E, September 1907, No. 98, NAI.

he would be obliged to take the opium back to Nepal[9]. The Nepalese envoy reached Chengtu on 11 October 1907. According to H.H. Fox, the acting British Consul-General at Chengtu, the Chinese provincial authorities of Chengtu treated the Nepalese envoy with scant courtesy, for the Nepalese *Kazi* was lodged in miserable quarters outside the North Gate. Mr. H.H. Fox called on the Nepalese envoy soon after his arrival at Chengtu and supplied the Nepalese envoy with English newspapers[10]. While in Singafu, on 10 February 1908 *Kazi* Bhairab Bahadur met the Dalai Lama, who was also on his way to Peking. The Nepalese mission most likely arrived at Peking by April, 1908. Here it should be mentioned that even before the arrival of the Nepalese mission in Peking, on 12 October 1907, through the British Resident J. Manners Smith, the Nepalese Prime Minister had sent to the British Legation in Peking a cover addressed to *Kazi* Bhairab Bahadur Gadhatola Chhetri, containing a draft for two thousand and twenty nine *Taels* equivalent to five thousand rupees in Indian currency[11]. Upon arrival of the Nepalese mission in Peking, Sir J.N. Jordan, the British Minister at Peking, delivered the draft to the Nepalese envoy. Besides that, the British Minister furnished the Nepalese envoy with newspapers from the British Legation and sent a number of his staff members to enquire about the Nepalese envoy's health. According to the British Minister, the Nepalese mission was lodged in the extreme north of the city of Peking, some four miles from the British Legation quarters, with somewhat inadequate accommodation, and guarded by an escort of Chinese troops which kept a careful watch on all comings and goings. The Russian Military Attache, Colonel L. Korniloff had

---

9 Translation of information received from *Kazi* Bhyrab Bahadur, 17 August 1907, Foreign Dept. Sec. E, March 1908, No. 1, NAI. The carrying of opium for trading purposes in China began with the Nepalese quinquennial mission of 1852.

10 H.H. Fox to J.Jordan, 25 November 1907, Foreign Dept. Sec. E, March 1908, No. 6, NAI.

11 J. Manners Smith to Secretary, Govt. of India, 12 October 1907, Foreign Dept. External B, January 1908, No. 92, NAI.

called upon the Nepalese delegation but was not received. The Nepalese envoy had informed the British Minister that he had instructions from the Nepalese Prime Minister to turn to the British Minister for assistance, if required, and as such he did not propose to establish relations with any other Legations[12].

The Nepalese delegation had its first audience with the Chinese Emperor on 24 April 1908. This took place in a courtyard of the Palace as *Kazi* Bhairab Bahadur and his suite (sixteen in number) were kneeling on one knee, while the Emperor was carried past them in his chair, apparently on his way to worship. The delegation was dressed in Nepalese uniforms. The presents which the delegates had brought for the Emperor were sent to the Palace on the following day. The Nepalese presents consisted of four elephant tusks, bales of cloth of gold, silk brocade and other stuffs, and spices. Two sets of official robes were subsequently presented to each member of the mission, one set for summer and the other for winter wear. *Kazi* Bhairab Bahadur's robes were of rich silk and the winter garments were lined with sable. The Nepalese envoy himself received the coral button of the first rank, and his suite the blue button[13].

The Nepalese mission's next audience with the Chinese Emperor took place early on the morning of 5 May 1908. On this occasion, the Empress Dowager was also present. The delegates did not enter the hall of audience in which the Imperial personages were seated, but advanced only as far as the foot of the steps leading up to the hall, and there knelt down on one knee, their eyes being, according to instructions, directed on the ground. The Emperor enquired about the health of His Highness the *Maharaja* and whether the mission had had a successful

12 J.N. Jordan to Edward Grey, 29 April 1908, Foreign Dept. Sec. E, October 1908, No. 705, NAI.

13 Memorandum of P. Grant Jones, 5 July 1908, Foreign Dept. Sec. E, October 1908, No. 711, NAI.

journey. *Kazi* Bhairab Bahadur, through his interpreter, returned favourable replies to His Majesty's queries, and the mission then withdrew. The ceremony of *Kowtow* was not performed and everything on this occasion was done strictly according to precedence. The Nepalese envoy complained to the British official, P. Grant Jones somewhat bitterly of Chinese conservatism, and seemed to imply that his exclusion from the actual presence was not entirely to his taste[14].

The Nepalese envoy *Kazi* Bhairab Bahadur called on British Minister Sir J. N. Jordan on 12 May 1908. A guard of honour of the 2nd Battalion Cameron Highlanders was called in to receive the Nepalese envoy at the main gate of the British Legation, and the British Minister received him in the drawing room with all the members of the Legation staff who were able to attend. According to the British Minister, *Kazi* Bhairab Bahadur was dressed in semi-European uniform and spoke fairly good English. During the course of the conversation, the Nepalese envoy described the principal incidents of his journey, his stay in Lhasa, his interview with the Dalai Lama at Singafu (His-An-Fu), and his halt at Chengtu in Szechuan, where, he said, he received much kindness at the hands of the Acting British Consul-General Mr. H.H. Fox. On 15 May 1908, Sir J.N. Jordan returned the Nepalese envoy's call. On 20 May 1908, at the invitation of Colonel J. H. Abbot Anderson, Commandant of the Legation Guard, the Nepalese envoy attended the International Legation guards Athletic Sports event which was held that year on the British Legation's grounds. This appeared to have been the Nepalese envoy's first meeting with other Europeans during his stay in Peking, as he had paid no calls, and did not propose to do so. On that occasion, the Nepalese envoy informed the British Minister that he had been commanded by the Nepalese Prime Minister to buy presents in Peking to be offered to the Nepalese King, and requested the British Minister's assistance in choosing them. According to Sir

---

14 *Ibid.*

J.N. Jordan, as the Nepalese envoy was suffering from the effects of his long journey, he gratefully accepted the British Minister's offer that he should be attended to by the medical officer of the Legation, Dr. Gray, who was to visit him on 21 May 1908[15].

Another meeting between the British Minister and the Nepalese envoy took place on 4 June 1908. During the conversation, *Kazi* Bhairab Bahadur stated that the question of continuing the Nepalese missions to China appeared to him to be of doubtful utility. Former missions had been largely in the nature of commercial speculations and had proved very successful in that respect. Little profit was now to be made by bringing Nepalese produce to China. The change, although the Nepalese envoy did not say so, was probably due to the restriction placed upon the sale of opium which was, the British Minister believed, in former years one of the articles in which the Nepalese mission traded. According to *Kazi* Bhairab Bahadur, the only advantage he saw in the continuance of the Nepalese missions to China was the opportunity it gave Nepal of gaining access to China and of acquiring some first-hand information of the great changes that were going on in China. The Nepalese envoy had utilized that opportunity to the best of his ability and had during his journey acquired a working knowledge of Chinese language in order to enable him to gain a better insight into the conditions of Chinese life. But, on the whole, *Kazi* Bhairab Bahadur was inclined to think that the mission was a relic of the past which might be discontinued, although the process should be a gradual one. It seems that the relations between the Nepalese envoy and the British Legation had been particularly cordial, for the British Legation provided medical attendance for the Nepalese envoy and one of his staff also underwent a minor operation in the British Legation hospital. Besides that, the British Minister had frequently

15 J.N. Jordan to Edward Grey, 25 May 1908, Foreign Dept. Sec. E, October 1908, No. 707, NAI.

designated for one of his staff, Mr. P. Grant Jones, to enquire about the health and comfort of the Nepalese envoy. Interestingly, the British Minister had also mentioned that he found it difficult, in view of the Nepalese envoy's scruples, to show him as much attention as he could have wished[16].

According to Sir J. N. Jordan, during his other interview with *Kazi* Bhairab Bahadur in July 1908, he found the Nepalese envoy less disposed than on a previous occasion to advocate the discontinuance of the Nepalese missions to China. The Nepalese envoy spoke of them as a "harmless and friendly practice" and considered them of some use in promoting friendly relations between Nepal and China in Tibet. While in Peking, *Kazi* Bhairab Bahadur took lessons in surveying from one of the British Legation's Indian surveyors with the view of making a road map of his journey on his way back to Nepal. According to the memorandum drawn up by the British Legation's staff Mr. P. Grant Jones, the Nepalese *Kazi* was anxious to set out on his return journey, as he found that the summer climate of Peking did not suit his health or that of the members of his retinue. The Nepalese envoy told Mr. Jones that the servants who attended to the mission while in Peking were all paid by the Chinese government, and he feared it was in the interest of their pockets to detain him in Peking as long as possible. According to Mr. Jones, the Nepalese envoy intended, however, to make inquiries of the Chinese officials, who occasionally visited him, as to the probable date of his farewell audience and the issue of his passport. To Mr. Jones, the Nepalese envoy expressed his deep gratitude for the various acts of kindness which he had received from the British Legation[17].

---

16 Same to Same, 5 June 1908, Foreign Dept. Sec. E, October 1908, No. 709, NAI.

17 Memorandum of P. Grant Jones, 5 July 1908, Foreign Dept. Sec. E, October 1908, No. 711, NAI.

Through *Kazi* Bhairab Bahadur's letter dated 6 August 1908, it seems that he had made an inquiry at the *Lifa Yamen* (an office) whether he could have two or three Chinese rifles on purchase, so that he might take them with him for the safety of himself and his party on the way during his return journey to Nepal. On 30 July 1908, some officials of the *Lifa Yamen* came to the Nepalese envoy's place, bringing with them four China-made magazine (five-Chambered) rifles, which, they said, were sent by the *Tunthan* of the *Yamen* by order of the Emperor as a present from His Majesty for the Nepalese mission's safety during its return journey. Of the four rifles, two which had long barrels were intended for *Kazi* Bhairab Bahadur, and the two others, viz. one long barreled and another short barreled (cavalry carbine), for *Sardar* Kahar Singh, the deputy leader of the Nepalese delegation. Those Chinese officials also informed the Nepalese envoy that the following day, i.e. 31 July 1908 had been appointed as the day for the Nepalese mission's leave taking with the Emperor, and that conveyances with an escort of Chinese officials would be ready at the Nepalese envoy's residence very early in the morning. Accordingly they came a little before daybreak, while it was still dark, with two foreign-made and eight Chinese-made carriages and escorted the Nepalese mission to Wansausan Palace where the Emperor was residing. On arrival there the Nepalese delegates were taken to a waiting room where the *Tunthan* and other officials were present. The Nepalese mission rested for a while there and when His Majesty came to the audience chamber, *Kazi* Bhairab Bahadur and *Sardar* Kahar Singh were ushered into his presence. At that time, the Emperor was seated on his throne and approaching near as the Nepalese *Kazi* and *Sardar* paid their respects to him, he said : "Convey my enquiries about health to the *Maharaja*. Do your journey comfortably". Both the Nepalese *Kazi* and *Sardar* paid their farewell respects to His Majesty and returned. The members of *Kazi* Bhairab Bahadur's retinue, i.e., *Subedars, Jamadars* and others, were told that as His Majesty was unwell they should pay their respects from the door of the Chamber, and they did accordingly. At the time of audience, the Emperor looked very weak and emaciated. After taking leave of the Emperor, the Nepalese envoy urged the *Lifa Yamen* for an early completion of the arrangement of the Nepalese mission's return journey[18]. During their five months stay in Peking, the Nepalese mission were granted four audiences by the Emperor[19].

On 11 September 1908, the Nepalese mission left Peking for Tientsin by a special train. According to the head of the Nepalese mission, *Kazi* Bhairab Bahadur, at the time of his departure, a guard of honour composed of twenty five soldiers with two officers besides those that were on sentry duty, was dispatched to the gate of his residence, and saluted as he passed. Just outside the gate a body of twenty four mounted soldiers also with two officers were ready to escort him to the railway station. Twelve of them rode in front and twelve behind him. As the Nepalese envoy passed through the main street of the city, crowds of spectators, among whom there were some Europeans, gathered at the place. On arrival at the railway station, *Kazi* Bhairab Bahadur found a guard of honour composed of one company with officers in full dress uniform drawn up on the platform. As he approached the railway carriage, Dr. Morrison met him and bade him a hearty good-bye. He also informed the Nepalese envoy of the return of the British Minister from Peticho to Peking and his intention to come to see him. No sooner had Dr. Morrison left than Sir J.N. Jordan, the British Minister, accompanied by his Secretary, Mr. Campbell, arrived at the place. *Kazi* Bhairab Bahadur took the British Minister to his railway carriage which was clean and nicely furnished. The interview was of a most cordial nature. Sir J.N. Jordan asked the Nepalese envoy as to why he was in a hurry to leave Peking

18 Translation of news received from *Kazi* Bhairab Bahadur, 6 August 1908, Foreign Dept. Sec. E, October 1908, No. 714, NAI.

19 Translation of *Kazi* Bhairab Bahadur's letter, 15 September 1908, Foreign Dept. Sec. E, January 1909, No. 413, NAI.

so soon and told him that he could have prolonged his stay there by a few days more. The Nepalese *Kazi* replied that his business at Peking was accomplished and that the earlier he started from the place the sooner he would reach home[20]. He also told the British Minister that he had obtained special permission from the Chinese government to pay a visit to Tientsin and to travel thence by train to Honan, whence he will proceed overland *via* Chengtu[21]. The Nepalese *Kazi* expressed to Sir J.N. Jordan his warm thanks for all his kindness to him which had added so much to his comfort during his stay at Peking. The British Minister wished the Nepalese envoy a comfortable journey. He also informed the Nepalese *Kazi* that he had written to the British Consuls at Tientsin and Thindafu (Chengtu), who would be pleased to afford the Nepalese envoy any necessary assistance. The Nepalese envoy thanked him saying that the British Minister's kindness will ever remain engraved in his mind. The British Minister looked quite cheerful and as it was time for the train to start he got up to take leave. *Kazi* Bhairab Bahadur got down to the platform and warmly shook hands with Sir J.N. Jordan. Soon after the train started and the guard of honour presented arms. It was half past one in the afternoon when the Nepalese mission departed for Tientsin[22]. According to the British Minister, at the time of leaving Peking, *Kazi* Bhairab Bahadur and the principal members of his staff were all dressed in Chinese official costume and wore the decorations which had been conferred upon them by the Emperor. Meanwhile, Sir J.N. Jordan had also remarked that a Chinese guard of honour was at the railway station, but no Chinese official of any standing was

---

20 *Ibid.*

21 Jordan to Edward Grey, 14 September 1908, Foreign Dept. Sec. E, January 1909, No. 411, NAI.

22 Translation of *Kazi* Bhairab Bahadur's letter, 15 September 1908, Foreign Dept. Sec. E, January 1909, No. 413, NAI.

present and the Nepalese envoy's departure, like his reception generally, was attended with scant ceremony[23].

From Peking it took the Nepalese mission four hours to reach Tientsin by train. Some Chinese officials sent by the local *Chundu* (Viceroy or Governor) were present at the railway platform there to receive the Nepalese mission. The British Consul-General of Tientsin had also taken the trouble to come and meet the Nepalese envoy in his railway carriage. After he had some talk with the British Consul-General concerning mutual welfare, the Nepalese envoy along with his retinue proceeded to the Tientsin city. While in Tientsin, the Nepalese *Kazi* called on the *Chundu* of Paochinfu and the British Consul-General. Besides that, he did some sight seeing in Tientsin. On 15 September 1908, the Nepalese mission left Tientsin for Honan *en route* to Thindafu by train[24]. On their arrival at Fusiang after leaving Singafu, the Nepalese mission heard the news of the death of the Emperor Kuang-hsu and the Dowager Empress as well as the accession of the new Emperor[25]. While in Thindafu, the Nepalese envoy met the British Consul-General, visited various government factories, bought four horses for himself, ten horses and other goods for the Nepalese Prime Minister. Regarding *Sardar* Kahar Singh's purchasing of twenty three horses, the Nepalese envoy had remarked that the *Chundu* of Thindafu did not like it and passed some remarks on it. The Nepalese mission left Thindafu on 5 February 1909 and reached Yutoofu on 21 February 1909. From Yutoofu, the Nepalese mission left for Tarchindeo (Tachienlu) on 25 February 1909[26]. On 7 May 1909, the Nepalese mission left Tarchindeo. The Nepalese mission after leaving Tarchindeo

---

23 Jordan to Edward Grey, 14 September 1908, Foreign Dept. Sec. E., January 1909, No. 411, NAI.

24 Translation of *Kazi* Bhairab Bahadur's letter, 15 September 1908, Foreign Dept. Sec. E, January 1909, No. 413, NAI.

25 Translation of a news-letter from *Kazi* Bhairab Bahadur, 7 February 1909, Foreign Dept. Sec. E, June 1909, No. 478, NAI.

26 *Ibid.*

proceeded on their journey without stopping anywhere except where horses and transportation for their use had to be changed. Travelling through Lithang and Bathang, the Nepalese mission finally reached Lhasa on 11 September 1909[27]. The Nepalese mission had brought with them about one hundred and eighty horses of different breeds known as "Chianta", "Pony", and "Siling". While in Lhasa, the Nepalese envoy met the Dalai Lama as well as the Chinese *Ambans* (Residents). The Nepalese mission seemed to have left Lhasa for Kathmandu around 21 January 1910[28].

Thus we see that the Indian Archival documents provide us much information about *Kazi* Bhairab Bahadur's mission to China. On the basis of the above discussed account of *Kazi* Bhairab Bahadur's mission to China, we can make the following concluding remarks. Firstly, it took *Kazi* Bhairab Bahadur twenty months to reach Peking from Kathmandu. Secondly, during his five months stay in Peking, the Nepalese envoy was granted audience by the Chinese Emperor for four times. Thirdly, *Kazi* Bhairab Bahadur's treatment in Peking was of the stereotyped kind which had been meted out to previous Nepalese missions since the last years of the eighteenth century. The Nepalese envoy presented the usual letter and presents from his sovereign to the Chinese Emperor. Fourthly, the Nepalese court had also sent opium with *Kazi* Bhairab Bahadur's mission to be sold in China. The Nepalese envoy hinted the British Minister that the Nepalese missions suffered a monetary loss by the new Chinese law of imposing severe restrictions on the sale of opium and as such, the future Nepalese missions would be of doubtful utility. This remark made by the head of the Nepalese mission was quite significant in that it soon resulted in the termination of the mission system itself. Finally, the Nepalese envoy *Kazi*

---

27 Chandra Shamsher to J. Manners Smith, 5 October 1909, Foreign Dept. Sec. E, October 1909, No. 716, NAI.

28 Translation of a letter from *Kazi* Bhairab Bahadur, 3 January 1910, Foreign Dept. Sec. E, March 1910, No. 431, NAI.

Bhairab Bahadur had developed a close rapport with Sir J.N. Jordan, the British Minister in Peking. The British Minister paid due attention to this *Kazi* Bhairab Bahadur's mission to China on their return journey, for which the Nepalese Prime Minister Chandra Shamsher thanked Sir J.N. Jordan. Besides that, in the annals of Sino-Nepalese relations the importance of *Kazi* Bhairab Bahadur's mission to China lies in the fact that it was the last Nepalese quinquennial mission to go to the Imperial Court of China. After nearly one hundred and fifteen years, the mission system was terminated, ending with this very mission.

***

The Alleged Dementia of the Nepalese Envoy *Kazi* Bhairab Bahadur*

The system of sending Nepalese quinquennial missions to China had its origin in the peace agreement of September, 1792 between Nepalese and Chinese officials following the ending of the Sino-Nepalese War of 1791-1792. From 1792 to 1906, Nepal sent altogether eighteen customary five-yearly missions to China. The mission system was finally terminated after 1906. The mission of 1906, i.e. the eighteenth and last Nepalese quinquennial mission to the Imperial Court of China, was led by *Kazi* Major Bhairab Bahadur Gadhatola Chhetri. This Nepalese delegation left Kathmandu on 10 August 1906 and reached Peking twenty months later, in April 1908. They remained in Peking for five months. After that, on 11 September 1908 they left Peking on the homeward journey, returning to Kathmandu by April 1910. There were reports on the strange conduct of the Nepalese envoy *Kazi* Bhairab Bahadur on his return journey to Nepal. Till now, no writer has discussed this topic on the basis of Indian archival documents[1]. As such, in

---

* Published in *Rolamba*, Vol. 15, No. 4 (October-December 1995), pp. 2-10.

1 W.N. Fergusson has given a short account of the strange behaviour of *Kazi* Bhairab Bahadur in Chingchihsien as narrated to him by C.H. Meares. Jnanmani Nepal has discussed this topic a bit based on Nepalese documents only. See W.N. Fergusson, *Land and People of Tibet and China in the Early Twentieth Century*, Delhi: Sharda Prakashan, Reprint, 1989, pp. 334-338, and Jnanmani Nepal, *Nepal-Bhot Chin Sambandhaka Kehi Sanskritik Paksha* (Some Cultural Aspects of Nepal-Tibet China Relations), Kathmandu: Royal Nepal Academy, 2045 B.S., pp, 391-393.

this paper an attempt is made to discuss the alleged strange conduct of the Nepalese envoy *Kazi* Bhairab Bahadur on his return journey to Nepal mainly based on the original unpublished documents preserved in the National Archives of India in New Delhi.

C.H. Meares' letter to Sir Walter Hilier as well as to the deputy-leader of the Nepalese mission of 1906, *Sardar* Kahar Singh Khadka's letter to the Nepalese court provides us with information regarding the strange conduct of the Nepalese envoy on his return journey to Nepal. Mr. C.H. Meares' letter dated 21 May 1909 to Sir Walter Hilier who placed the letter at the disposal of Sir J.N. Jordan, the British Minister at Peking, gives us information about the state of *Kazi* Bhairab Bahadur's health[2]. Mr Meares had also described the strange conduct of the Nepalese envoy to W.N. Fergusson[3]. Now let us discuss Mr. Meares' report in detail. According to C.H. Meares, upon his arrival at a place called Chingchihsien, where the Tachienlu road joined the Ningyuanfu road, he found that the Nepalese envoy, with a retinue of several hundred followers, Chinese and Nepalese, had occupied all the big houses. Therefore he had to get a small place about half a mile a far away. After having supper, Mr. Meares went and called on the Nepalese envoy and had an interesting time. He found the Nepalese envoy a very pleasant old gentleman who spoke perfect English. The next morning, before daybreak, Mr. Meares went to see off his caravan, and when he reached the door of the inn, he found the Nepalese envoy waiting to see him. He found the Nepalese envoy there in his night clothes. At that time he was attended by one Nepalese servant who held a saddled horse. As soon as the Nepalese envoy saw Mr. Meares, he threw his arms round Mr. Meares' neck and began to cry bitterly saying that he was dying. The Nepalese envoy declared that in the night the Chinese

2. J.N. Jordan to Edward Grey, 31 May 1909, Foreign Dept. Secret E, September 1909, No. 16, National Archives of India(NAI), New Delhi.
3 Fergusson, f.n. no. 1, pp. 334-338.

and his own Nepalese people had tried to kill him with chloroform, and that they were conspiring to poison him, and had been drugging his food for several days. He begged for Meares' protection as an Englishman, and insisted that Meares should take him back to Chengtu and turn him over to the British Consul. Meares then took the Nepalese envoy to his (Meares') room and offered him some food which the Nepalese *Kazi* ate, though it was quite contrary to his caste laws. Shortly afterwards some of his Nepalese officials arrived, but as soon as the Nepalese envoy saw them he seized a revolver and tried to shoot them. With some difficulty Mr. Meares managed to get the revolver from him and pacified him.

A little later a Chinese official came to see the Nepalese envoy, but he at once seized a big wooden hammer that was lying in the room and tried to kill him. Just managing to catch the Nepalese envoy in time, Mr. Meares tried to pacify the Nepalese *Kazi* until he got the Chinese official safely out of the house. After the Chinese official left, he grew much quieter and told Mr. Meares many interesting things about himself and his country. By that time he seemed more composed. Leaving the Nepalese envoy in charge of his (Meares') head servant, Mr. Meares slipped out of the room and went to the telegraph office to send a wire to the British Consul at Chengtu, stating the case and asking what steps he should take, saying that the Nepalese envoy insisted on returning with him to Chengtu. Mr. Meares received the reply that the British Consul had left Chengtu. Then he went to the inn where the Nepalese envoy was lodging. There he found the envoy's officers in a great state of agitation. They could only speak Hindi; but fortunately Mr. Meares was able to talk to them, and found them all to be very nice men. They said that they were quite sure that the envoy was out of his mind, and that they could do nothing with him. They also told Mr. Meares that none of them ever thought of killing the envoy as it would mean death to all of them and they asked Mr. Meares to telegraph the Nepalese Prime Minister for instructions on what they were to do. So the British gentleman wrote out a long telegram saying that the envoy was acting strangely and insisted on returning to Chengtu, and asking what the delegates were to do. He took that telegram to the office but the clerk said that he did not know where Nepal was, or how much the telegram would cost, until he received particulars from Chengtu. He then went back and talked to the envoy for a long time trying to persuade him that his people had no intention of killing him and trying to get him back to his own house. Finally in the evening the Nepalese envoy got calmer, and Mr. Meares got all the envoy's people to come up to his inn to see the envoy and swore on their scriptures to protect the envoy. They told the envoy that if he insisted on leaving the delegation, they would never dare to return to Nepal, and that they would all disperse and become religious mendicants. After a lot of persuasion the envoy agreed to do what Mr. Meares recommended, and finally decided to continue his journey to Tachienlu, where he would find other Europeans as well as a foreign doctor, and would stay there for some time. Then Mr. Meares escorted the Nepalese envoy back to his inn and stayed with him till late at night. The envoy gave the British gentleman some presents and a photograph of himself, and begged him to take any of the ponies he fancied. But Mr. Meares insisted that as he was leaving the country, he did not need any of them. They were all most anxious that Mr. Meares should accompany them on their journey along the southern road to Lhasa, where they were to stay a month before going on to Kathmandu. To Meares it was the chance of a lifetime; but he had other work to do and had to refuse their offer, and slipped back to his inn[4]. While describing his meeting with the Nepalese envoy in detail, Mr. Meares also made the following remark: "It is possible that he (the envoy) was foxing as the Chinese were treating him badly, that is, with no respect; and he dreaded the long overland journey. It certainly was the hardest contract to settle I ever met, if I had not known their talk I do not know what would have

4 *Ibid.*, J.N. Jordan to Edward Grey, 31 May 1909, Foreign Dept. Sec. E, September 1909, No. 16, NAI.

happened"[5]. Here it should be mentioned that even Kahar Singh Khadka, the *Sardar* of the Nepalese mission, who was the officer second in rank to *Kazi* Bhairab Bahadur, had informed the Nepalese Prime Minister Chandra Shamsher that "all was not right" with *Kazi* Bhairab Bahadur[6].

After obtaining Meares' letter through Sir Walter Hillier, the British Minister Sir J.N. Jordan telegraphed the acting British Consul-General at Chengtu instructing him to make enquiries as to the alleged dementia of the Nepalese envoy who was on his return journey to Nepal. From the information obtained by Smith, the acting British Consul-General at Chengtu, it would appear that the Nepalese envoy, travelling through Chinchihsien and Tachienlu reached Litang, which he left on 3 June 1909 in an apparently satisfactory state of health and arrived on 10 June 1909 at Batang quite well[7]. In the face of these reports from the acting British Consul-General at Chengtu, it becomes rather difficult to estimate the amount of credibility to be attached to the report of C.H. Meares. Sir J.N. Jordan did not doubt the sincerity of Mr. Meares[8]. In spite of that, it remained questionable as to whether Mr. Meares exaggerated the incident due to his imaginative and excitable temparament, whether the Nepalese envoy was really demented at the time and had since recovered, or whether the envoy was acting a part for his own purposes. It was reported again that the Nepalese envoy's health had deteriorated after his arrival at Chamdo, which lies between Batang and Lhasa. The Nepalese *Kazi* appeared to have abandoned charge of the mission and marched separately with a few followers ahead of the main party towards Lhasa. It was also reported that the Nepalese

---

5 J.N. Jordan to Edward Grey, 31 May 1909, Foreign Dept. Sec. E, September 1909, No. 16, NAI.

6 J. Manners Smith to Secretary, Govt. of India, 20 July-21 July 1909, Foreign Dept. Sec. E, September 1909, No.19, NAI.

7 J.N. Jordan to Edward Grey, 23 June 1909, Foreign Dept. Sec. E, September 1909, No.20, NAI.

8 *Ibid.*

envoy had taken to carrying a Tibetan prayer-wheel which he revolved as if he were a Buddhist and not a Hindu. Because of that the Nepalese Prime Minister had sent instructions to Major Captain Jit Bahadur Khatri Chhetri, the Nepalese *Vakil*(envoy) at Lhasa, with a letter to Tibetan authorities requesting them to recognize the Nepalese *Sardar* Kahar Singh Khadka as head of the Nepalese mission in place of *Kazi* Bhairab Bahadur. This letter the Nepalese *Vakil* was to make use of if he found that *Kazi* Bhairab Bahadur was not fit to complete his duties[9]. But by the time of the arrival of the Nepalese mission in Lhasa on 11 September 1909, the Nepalese envoy *Kazi* Bhairab Bahadur seemed to have been in a satisfactory state of health. It was evidenced by the fact that after the arrival of the Nepalese mission in Lhasa, the Nepalese *Vakil* did not report anything unusual in the Nepalese envoy's behaviour and that *Kazi* Bhairab Bahadur's own letters to the Nepalese Prime Minister were lucid and intelligent[10]. Moreover, according to *Kazi* Bhairab Bahadur's letter to the Nepalese Prime Minister, the Nepalese envoy, in the capacity of the leader of the Nepalese mission to China, met the Dalai Lama and the Chinese *Ambans*(Residents) at Lhasa on 27 December 1909 and 31 December 1909 respectively[11].

Now the question arises as to whether the reports regarding the breakdown of *Kazi* Bhairab Bahadur's health and his desertion of the mission was actually exaggerated or not. On the basis of the information provided by the British Minister, Sir J.N. Jordan and the Nepalese Prime Minister Chandra Shamsher, let us examine the facts about the reported strange conduct of the Nepalese envoy *Kazi* Bhairab Bahadur on his return journey to Nepal. Here it should be mentioned that soon

---

9 J.Manners Smith to Secretary, Govt. of India, 23 - 24 September 1909, Foreign Dept. Sec. E, October 1909, No.715, NAI.

10 Same to Same, 6 October 1909, Foreign Dept. Sec. E, October 1909, No. 716, NAI.

11 Same to Same, 2 February 1909, Foreign Dept. Sec. E, March 1910, No. 431, NAI.

after he left Kathmandu for Lhasa, the Nepalese envoy had fallen ill in Shigatse and after reaching Gyantse on 16 October 1906, he received British medical attention[12]. Next, on his arrival in Peking in April 1908, the Nepalese envoy was visibly suffering from the effects of his twenty months of travelling[13], and he was attended to during his stay in Peking by the medical officer of the British legation. In conversation with the British Minister, Sir J.N. Jordan, the Nepalese envoy had attributed his ill-health largely to the worry and discomfort effected by the neglect and poor treatment of which he had been the victim *en route* at the hands of the minor Chinese officials whose duty it was to afford him transport facilities. The envoy's difficulties seemed to have started only when he reached the borders of China proper. Besides that, while reporting to the British Minister in Peking, the acting British Consul-General at Chengtu had also stated that the Nepalese envoy was complaining of difficulties of a similar nature on his return journey as well[14]. So these troubles seemed to have doubtless contributed, as much as the physical stress of the journey, and affected the state of the Nepalese envoy's health as mentioned by Meares and the Nepalese *Sardar* Kahar Singh Khadka. According to the private letter of a missionary received at the British Consul in Chengtu, the missionary met the Nepalese envoy at Batang on the evening of 10 June 1909, on the day of the Nepalese envoy's arrival in Batang. The missionary stated

---

12 Diary of Lieutenant F.M. Bailey, Officiating British Trade Agent at Gyantse, 20 October-27 October 1906, Foreign Dept. Sec. E, July 1907, Nos. 304-305, NAI.

13 The British Minister, Sir J.N. Jordan had wrongly noted that the Nepalese mission took eighteen months to reach Peking. But the fact is that the Nepalese mission took twenty months to reach Peking, for it left Kathmandu on 10 August 1906 and reached Peking in April 1908. See J.Manners Smith to Secretary, Govt. of India, 17 August 1906, Foreign Dept. Sec. E, September 1906, No. 263. NAI, and J.N. Jordan to Edward Grey, 29 April 1908, Foreign Dept. Sec. E, October 1908, No. 705, NAI.

14 J.N. Jordan to Edward Grey, 31 May 1909, Foreign Dept. Sec. E, September 1909, No. 16, NAI.

that at the time of his meeting, the Nepalese envoy appeared to be in good health, and talked freely of his experiences at Chinchihsien, where he said that Meares saved his life by giving him some coffee and sugar. *Kazi* Bhairab Bahadur's men told the missionary that the problem had not recurred, and that they would see that the envoy would not suffer from such things from then on[15]. Thus it would appear from the missionary's letter that at the time of his meeting with Meares, the Nepalese envoy was merely suffering from a nervous attack resulting from his physical indisposition. Here it should be also noted that after his meeting with Meares in Chinchihsien, the Nepalese envoy went to Tachienlu from whence he wrote a letter dated 7 May 1909 to the Nepalese Prime Minister. Upon examining that letter, it seems that the envoy was quite well[16], for his letter was clear and intelligent and marked by cordial references to Europeans, i.e. the British Consuls and missionaries whom he had met *en route* during his return journey to Nepal overland *via* Chengtu. Thus it seems that the Nepalese envoy's breakdown at Chinchihsien was possibly a temporary incident and was due to alcohol or drugs, or to suffering from a nervous attack resulting from his physical indisposition.

As to the Nepalese *Sardar* Kahar Singh Khadka's report regarding the strange conduct of the Nepalese envoy as well as his having abandoned charge of the mission and marching separately with a few followers ahead of the main party towards Lhasa, the Nepalese Prime Minister Chandra Shamsher attributed it to ill-feeling, as he was aware that the officers of the mission were not "pulling well together"[17]. It was said that the Nepalese Prime Minister regarded *Kazi* Bhairab Bahadur, who had a good knowledge of English and some working

---

15 Same to Same, 3 August 1909, Foreign Dept. Sec. E, September 1909, No. 713, NAI.

16 Chandra Shumsher to J. Manners Smith, 4 July 1909, Foreign Dept. Sec. E, September 1909, No. 18, NAI.

17 J.Manners Smith to Secretary, Govt. of India, 20 July-21 July 1909, Foreign Dept. Sec. E, September 1909, No. 19, NAI.

knowledge of Chinese, to be an astute politician. Perhaps due to this reason, the Nepalese Premier did not fully trust the Nepalese envoy. That is why he seemed to have designated *Sardar* Kahar Singh primarily to observe the activities of *Kazi* Bhairab Bahadur. Once the Nepalese envoy discovered this, his terms with *Sardar* Kahar Singh did not remain cordial. It was reported that their relationship became strained mainly after their arrival in Peking. While in Peking, *Sardar* Kahar Singh sent a letter to the Nepalese Premier in which he accused the *Kazi* of misappropriating an amount of more than nineteen thousand and five hundred rupees[18]. Likewise, on their return journey to Nepal, he also reported to the Nepalese Prime Minister about all sorts of strange behaviour on the part of the Nepalese envoy. In the meantime, it should also be mentioned that while in Peking, *Kazi* Bhairab Bahadur's proposal to introduce Chinese language instruction in Nepal by opening a school especially for this purpose was not certainly appreciated by his master, the Nepalese Premier. The *Kazi* was well aware of the fact. Besides that, the Nepalese Premier's appointment of *Sardar* Kahar Singh especially for the purpose of observing all of the *Kazi's* activities and *Sardar* Kahar Singh's reporting from Peking about the Nepalese envoy's alleged misappropriation of money too may have contributed to bring about the state of the *Kazi's* health as described by *Sardar* Kahar Singh. Under the circumstances mentioned above, one finds difficult to accept totally the reportings of *Sardar* Kahar Singh.

Thus from the foregoing description, it is difficult to ascertain the facts regarding the affairs of *Kazi* Bhairab Bahadur. It seems that most probably *Kazi* Bhairab Bahadur temporarily suffered from nervous attacks resulting from physical indisposition due to the strain of the long and ardous journey, or due to the worry and discomfort occasioned by the neglect and poor treatment of which he had been the victim *en route* at the hands of the minor Chinese officials or due to his

---

18 Nepal, f.n. 1., pp. 450-454.

ill-feelings toward *Sardar* Kahar Singh. As such, under such circumstances it may be assumed that Meares and Nepalese *Sardar* Kahar Singh may have exaggerated the whole affair extremely. Last but not the least, the possibility cannot be ruled out that *Kazi* Bhairab Bahadur may have been "bluffing", as the Chinese were treating him badly, that is, with no respect.

***

The Opium Trade and the Nepalese Quinquennial Missions to China*

Nepal's sending quinquennial missions to China after the Nepal-Tibet-China War of 1792 continued up to 1906. Two noteworthy features of the Nepalese quinquennial mission system were: (a) Nepal successively sent altogether thirteen quinquennial missions to China for the first sixty years (1792-1852), and that they reached the Chinese capital, Peking, and returned home in time as scheduled, normally taking around two years, (b) after the Nepal- Tibet War of 1855-1856, the system of sending Nepalese missions to China became quite irregular, for during the fifty-four year period (1852-1906), Nepal despatched only five missions to China. Besides that, from that period on, the nature of the Nepalese mission became more commercial and less political. Because of this, the duration of the Nepalese missions became quite a bit longer. With the hope of doing profitable trade in China, the ruling Rana families of Nepal did not hesitate to push the Nepalese delegates into the illegal opium trade. So the Nepalese missions stayed in China for a longer period in order to sell opium and other tradable goods, as directed by the ruling Rana family. The 1852 Nepalese mission inaugurated the system of carrying opium to sell in China, and the system continued till the last Nepalese mission to China in 1906. The main objective of this paper is to describe the involvement of the Rana family in the opium trade during quinquennial missions to China.

---

* Unpublished Paper.

Jang Bahadur, the founder of the Rana system in Nepal, initiated the technique of making a large profit by involving the Nepalese political missions to China in the opium trade. Apparently he was very well aware of the fact that following the opium war of 1839-1842, the opium trade in China continued to grow, and perhaps through the 1847 Nepalese mission to China, he might have received information regarding the wide spread prevalence of opium smoking in China as well as the demand for opium in the Chinese market following the opium war. Besides that, he also knew that the goods belonging to the Nepalese missions not only could be carried freely from the Nepalese border to Peking and back but they were also allowed to pass with diplomatic immunity. Such diplomatic privileges accorded to the Nepalese mission, along with the prospect of a lot of profitable trade through opium may have prompted Jang Bahadur to involve the Nepalese mission in the opium trade. With all these considerations, he gave his approval for the 1852 Nepalese mission, under the leadership of *Kazi* Gambhir Singh Adhikari, to carry a lot of commodities for trading purposes, including nearly three *lakh* (Rs. 3,00, 000) rupees, worth of opium duty free, with the diplomatic privilege to sell them in China in spite of its legal ban in that country[1]. It was also reported that the immense quantity of opium being smuggled into China was sold at high prices[2]. But unfortunately, while returning from Peking, the Nepalese mission was reported to have been rudely treated by the Chinese authorities and the people of eastern Tibet. While reporting to the Secretary, Govt. of India on 6 May 1854, G. Ramsay, the British Resident in Nepal, stated that on several occasions Jang Bahadur told him that he (Jang Bahadur) and his brothers were in a state of great anxiety about the 1852 mission, for they had smuggled into China by their means, three *lakhs* (Rs. 3,00,000) rupees worth

1 Ramsay to Secretary, Govt. of India, 6 May 1854, Foreign Dept. Sec. 26 May 1854, No. 50, National Archives of India (NAI), New Delhi.

2 Same to Same, 29 July 1867, Foreign Dept. Polt. A, August 1867, No. 53, NAI.

of opium together with pearls. The British Resident had also reported that just after the 1852 Nepalese mission left the Nepalese capital, Jang Bahadur professed to have sent up only a very few thousand worth of opium (by then he said at least two *Lakhs* (Rs. 2,00,000) worth) and that he prevented his brothers and the *Sirdars* from adding a much larger quantity to that for fear of detection and disgrace. Meanwhile the British Resident also interestingly remarked that he was disposed to credit Jang Bahadur's admission as being more in accordance with the Nepalese character. He went on to say as such: "The large sum of money the proceeds of the sale of all this smuggled property should now be in the charge of Lieutenant (Bhimsen Rana), who may perhaps have been playing false, and have proved unable to resist the temptation of enriching himself, and who could, easily find partisans amongst the notoriously corrupt and venal Chinese officials in Tibet. It is not at all improbable that he may have appropriated to himself this large sum of money and that the despatch of troops towards Lassa is in order to recover it-but, this is mere surmise on my part, or, the Chinese authorities knowing as they necessarily must do how large a treasure is in his custody may have exacted heavy payments from him, and perhaps detained him (the mission is now several months over due) on his refusing to comply with their demands"[3]. From the foregoing account it seems that perhaps the rough attitude towards the 1852 Nepalese mission may have been due to its smuggling activities. It appears that the 1852 Nepalese mission, which carried a huge amount of opium under diplomatic privileges, had aroused suspicion among the Chinese authorities, who did not like the entry of contraband objects, that is, opium in their country. It seems that although the Chinese authorities did not react immediately, but indirectly, they may have deliberately mistreated the 1852 Nepalese mission on its return journey. Whatever the case may be, it is a historical fact that Nepal's opium trade in China seemed to have commenced with

3 Same to Same, 6 May 1854, Foreign Dept. Sec. 26 May 1854, No. 50, NAI.

the mission of 1852, and that due to the illtreatment of the 1852 Nepalese mission, not only did Nepal stop dispatching missions to China until 1866, but it also became one of the important factors which ultimately led to the outbreak of the Nepal-Tibet War of 1855-1856.

Here it should be pointed out that it was after the receipt of several overtures from the Chinese *Amban* (Resident) at Lhasa inviting him to reestablish the relations that formerly existed between China and Nepal, and promising upon the part of the Emperor that any future mission that may be sent to him by Nepal shall be received with high honour and consideration, that Jang Bahadur decided in June 1866 to send a mission to Peking[4]. One important factor which seemed to have prompted Jang Bahadur to dispatch a mission to Peking was the great profit coming out of the mission's trading activities, especially the opium trade in China. Thus after a lapse of fourteen years, Nepal sent her mission to China in 1866. The mission was led by *Kazi* Jagat Sher Sijapati, the son of Colonel Lal Singh Sijapati. The Nepalese mission, which left Kathmandu on 2 August, 1866[5], was only able to reach Ta Tsin Deo (Tachienlu), about half way to Peking, near the China-Tibet border, where it waited for nearly two years for permission to proceed to Peking. This mission was greatly humiliated when it was not allowed to visit Peking due to a Muslim rebellion in Western China. Like the previous mission, this 1866 Nepalese mission suffered several hardships, including the death of several of its delegates. Likewise, on that occasion too, Jang Bahadur and his brothers had sent a lot of merchandise with the mission, including a huge quantity of opium valued at four and a

---

4 Same to Same, 9 June 1866, Foreign Dept. Polt. A, June 1866, No. 163, NAI.

5 For details of the 1866 Nepalese mission, See Ministry of Foreign Affairs(MFA), Kathmandu, Poka No. Pa 64. Ramsay to Secretary, Govt. of India, 7 August 1866, Foreign Dept. Polt A. August 1866, No. 104, NAI. But Sever has wrongly stated that the Nepalese mission left Kathmandu on 15 August 1866. See Adrian Sever, *Aspects of Modern Nepalese History,* New Delhi: Vikas Publishing House Pvt. Ltd., 1995, p. 170.

half *lakhs* (Rs. 4,50,000) rupees, for sale in China. Besides Jang Bahadur and his brothers, a Newar merchant and monopolist by the name of *Sahu* Dharma Narayan Manandhar[6] had also sent with this 1866 Nepalese mission one of his nephews who carried a vast quantity of opium, cloth, spices and other goods[7]. But as no market was found, it was deposited at the Nepalese godowns at Lhasa and the Nepalese were at a loss for not being able to dispose them. It was reported that as half of the amount of opium carried by the 1866 Nepalese mission proved unsaleable, the remaining opium, consisting of four hundred coolies (porters) loads, was brought back to Lhasa by the Nepalese mission[8]. Furthermore it was also reported that upwards of a *lakh* (Rs. 1,00,000) rupees worth of opium and valuable goods carried by the mission of 1866 were destroyed due to the inclement weather they experienced while traversing the numerous snowy passes and mountains between the Nepalese and Chinese borders[9]. Captain Jit Man Singh Khatri Chhetri, the Nepalese *Vakil* (envoy) at Lhasa, could sell only half of the opium brought back by the Nepalese mission at

---

6 Dharma Narayan Manandhar (Sayami), besides being a very prominent rich merchant of his period, was a close associate of Jang Bahadur and had also performed the *Samyak Puja* ceremony. See Jit Bahadur Manandhar, *"Dhamana Sayami", Smarika (Souvenir),* Published in Newari (*Nepal Bhasa*) by Kendriya Manandhar Sangha (Central Manandhar Association), 1115 Nepal Sambat (2051 B.S.), pp. 22-28.
See also Vijay Kumar Manandhar, "*Sahu* Dharma Narayan Manandhar: A Financier And Member of the Bureaucratic Elite of the Nineteenth Century", *Voice of History*, Vol. XIV, No. 1 (June 1999), pp. 19-36.

7 Ramsay to Secretary, Govt. of India, 29 July 1867, Foreign Dept. Polt. A., August 1867, No. 53, NAI.

8 Daniel Wright, Officiating Resident to Secretary, Govt. of India, 27 February 1875, Foreign Polt. A, May 1875, No. 104, NAI. Uprety has mistakenly referred to the 1866 mission as the 1875 mission which could not dispose of the opium, and that four hundred coolie loads of opium had to be brought back to Lhasa, for the Nepalese mission could not even reach Peking. See Prem R. Uprety, *Nepal-Tibet Relations 1850-1930,* Kathmandu: Puga Nara, 1980, p. 165.

9 Ramsay to Secretary, Govt. of India, 29 July 1867, Foreign Dept. Polt. A, August 1867, No. 53, NAI.

Lhasa, and the remaining half was brought back to the Nepalese capital before it could be sold at a much lower price to the Indian government[10]. In this way it can be well assumed that the Chinese government's harsh attitude towards the 1866 Nepalese mission by refusing them permission to proceed to Peking was mainly due to their opium smuggling activities. Here it should be mentioned that although the Chinese authorities did not directly react immediately in 1852, but at the time of the 1866 Nepalese mission, they did not allow the mission, which had carried a large quantity of opium for sale in China to proceed to Peking from Tachienlu merely because of a Muslim rebellion in western China.

Mr. T.T. Cooper, the English traveller in China who met the Nepalese mission of 1866 in Tibet, was also under the impression that the Nepalese mission's progress to Peking had been arrested for having possessed opium[11]. According to T.T. Cooper, after much persuasion, *Kazi* Jagat Sher was allowed to proceed as far as Chen-tu in order to dispose of several chests of opium brought for sale in China. The Nepalese envoy soon reached Chen-tu, and hoped to proceed further, but the Chinese authorities made that impossible; he could have neither coolies nor boats, and , what was worse, no one would buy his opium; it was too strong, and the people preferred the native drug. Interestingly, while reporting about the 1866 Nepalese mission to Hugh Fraser, British Charge d' Affaires at Peking, E.C. Baber, British Consular officer at Chunking, had remarked that the Nepalese missions were little more than disguised trade ventures, and that the Chinese feared that the Nepalese missions would sooner or later develop into a commercial establishment

---

10 Kanchanmoy Mojumdar, *Anglo-Nepalese Relations in the Nineteenth Century,* Calcutta: Firma K.L. Mukhopadhyay, 1973, p. 112.

11 R.C. Lawrence to C.U. Aitchison, 10 September 1870, Foreign Dept. Sec. I, 1870, No. 400, NAI.

in western China[12]. Thus from the foregoing description it can be clearly stated that the main reason why the 1866 Nepalese mission was sent back by the Chinese at Tachienlu, of the Chinese province of Szechuwan, seemed mainly due to the large quantity of opium the Rana authorities had sent with it and which, ordinarily would have been sold free of duty and taxes as a privilege granted to the mission. Importantly enough, R.C. Lawrence, the British Resident in Nepal, had also stated that he met *Kazi* Jagat Sher, the leader of the 1866 Nepalese mission, upon its return to Kathmandu, and the Nepalese *Kazi* handed over his travel diary to him (the British Resident).

In his diary, *Kazi* Jagat Sher had interestingly enough referred to the important subject of the cultivation of opium in China, and in conversation with the British Resident, the Nepalese envoy dwelt strongly upon it. *Kazi* Jagat Sher said that the drug was most extensively cultivated in the province of Se-Chuen (Szechuwan), the whole country appearing as a field of poppy heads. Furthermore the British Resident had also remarked that the fact was that the Nepalese government was much interested in the subject, having suffered a heavy pecuniary loss as a result of the revival of the cultivation of the poppy in the southern, introduction into the western districts of China[13]. Interestingly enough in his travel account, *Kazi* Jagat Sher, while describing the Chinese country Wass-ko, commented about the cultivation of opium in China at a great length: "The cultivation of opium in the whole of the western district of China is now very large. After the drug is extracted and the oil for culinary purposes, the seeds are ground down into flour and the stalks used as fuel. The indigenous opium, though far inferior to the foreign, is universally preferred on account of the difference in price. The people are afraid to touch

---

12 E.C. Baber, Consular officer at Chungking to Hugh Fraser, Her Majesty's Charge d' Affaires at Peking, 2 August 1878, Foreign Dept. Sec., December 1878, No. 27, NAI.

13 R.C. Lawrence to C.U. Aitchison, 10 September 1870, Foreign Dept. Sec. I, 1870, No. 400, NAI.

the foreign drug, as, once habituated to it, they would not be satisfied with their own. The rice (rich) alone use it to strengthen the country stuff. Till recently the Tibetans used to import the Bengal opium, the product of the Nipal Teraie (Nepal Tarai), but this has almost ceased, as the area under cultivation in China has increased and is increasing, and the Thibetans draw their supplies from thence. The Thibetans and Chinese use the opium for smoking"[14].

Here it should be pointed out that the extreme discourtesy meted out by the Chinese officials in Chen-tu and the deaths of several members of the 1866 Nepalese mission in eastern Tibet led Jang Bahadur to think seriously about not sending any further missions at all, but the lure of huge commercial profits, especially through the opium trade, was too strong to resist, for the Nepalese missions had long ceased to have any political significance and had assumed the character of lucrative trading ventures. This is because the Nepalese ruling elite were well aware of the fact that in spite of all odds and all sorts of harrassment by the Chinese officials, the five-yearly mission system indeed provided a golden opportunity for them to dispose of a considerable cargo of opium in the western provinces of China without paying the heavy maritime duty and "lekin" taxes[15]. As such, Jang Bahadur decided to despatch the next mission to Peking in 1877[16]. But before the mission could be sent to China, Jang Bahadur died on 25 February, 1877 and was succeeded by his brother Ranaudip Singh who sent the Nepalese mission to China in July 1877. This 1877 Nepalese mission was led by *Kazi* Tej Bahadur Rana, a cousin of

14 Same to Same, 10 September 1870, Foreign Dept. Sec. I, 1870, No. 401, NAI.

15 Proposed Mission from Nipal to China, Foreign Dept. Sec. E, September 1876, Nos. 129-133, NAI.

16 Memorial from Sugn Kwei, Acting Resident in Tibet, published in the Peking Gazette, 11 May, 1876, Foreign Dept. Sec. E, September 1876, No. 130, NAI.

Ranaudip Singh[17]. Once again, as with the 1866 Nepalese mission, the Chinese authorities tried to stop the Nepalese mission of 1877, and thus did not allow the mission to proceed to Peking. Here it should be noted that the Chinese government had earlier given the 1877 Nepalese mission permission to proceed to the Chinese capital. But later on, the Chinese authorities stopped the mission at Tachienlu, a Chinese town on the Tibetan border, and asked them to surrender the presents and return from there. It seems that the Chinese greatly suspected that the 1877 Nepalese mission, too was carrying opium along with other merchandise, and that the Chinese did not at all like the Nepalese mission's involvement in the opium trade. That is why, similar to the 1866 mission, this time too, the Chinese stopped the Nepalese mission once again at Tachienlu with the intention of preventing the Nepalese mission's visit to Peking, explaining that it was "owing to the interrruption of communication along the post roads caused by the unusually severe famine in the provinces of Shansi and Shensi"[18]. Later on, although the Nepalese mission was allowed to visit Peking only at the insistence of the Nepalese government, the Chinese (who were truly dissatisfied with the arrival of the Nepalese mission in Peking), left no stone unturned to humiliate them. For it was reported that not only were the members lodged in the dirty buildings assigned to the tributary missions[19], but also the leader and the higher officials of the mission received audience in the Ch'ing court as 'Vassals' [20]. Besides that the Chinese officer in charge of the mission even attempted to prevent the mission from meeting the British

---

17 For details of the 1877 Nepalese mission, See MFA, Poka No. Pa 64, F.Henvey, Officiating Resident in Nepal to T.H. Thornton, Secretary, Govt. of India, 15 July 1877, Foreign Dept. Sec., October 1877, No. 149, NAI.

18 Peking Gazette, 24 March 1879, Foreign Dept. Sec. , June 1879, No. 23, NAI.

19 T.F. Wade, Her Majesty's Minister at Peking to Viceroy of India, 16 January 1880, Foreign Dept. Polt. A, April 1880, No. 98, NAI.

20 Her Majesty's Minister at Peking to Ripon, Viceroy of India, 1 November 1880, Foreign Polt. A., January 1881, No. 84, NAI

representative at Peking. It appears that the Chinese seemed to have taken all these measures in order to harrass or humiliate the Nepalese mission, whom the Chinese believed to be engaging in opium-trading (smuggling) activities. Thus considering the Chinese response it can be assumed that the 1877 Nepalese mission too was carrying a large quantity of opium for sale in China; if not, the Chinese would not have humiliated the Nepalese mission. Besides that, Sir T.F. Wade, the British Minister at Peking who met the leader of the 1877 Nepalese mission, interestingly remarked that the leader of the Nepalese mission did not like to say that the object of the mission was commercial, but the British Minister took it to be in reality. The British Minister had further remarked that like most missions from other countries to China, the Nepalese mission had brought various articles, some, of course, to be presented as gifts to the Ch'ing Emperor, but the rest for sale[21]. Here it should be noted that since the time of the 1852 Nepalese mission, opium had emerged as the most profitable trading item of the mission. In this way it seems that the 1877 Nepalese mission was also involved in opium trading activities and, due to that factor, the journey of the mission became significantly longer; this mission returned home after nearly five years. Normally, the Nepalese mission to China took around two years to complete the journey.

Nepal sent her next mission to China in 1886 under the leadership of *Kazi* Ran Bikram Rana, the eldest son of Colonel Tej Bahadur Rana, who had led the previous Nepalese mission of 1877[22]. This mission too seemed to have been involved in

---

21 T.F. Wade to Viceroy of India, 16 January 1880, Foreign Dept. Polt. A., April 1880, No. 98, NAI.

22 For details of the 1886 mission, See MFA, Poka No. Pa 64, Girdlestone to H.M. Durand, Secretary to the Govt. of India, 15 September 1886, Foreign Sec. E., October 1886, No. 1, NAI. See also, "Nepal Desh Ko Itihas" (History of Nepal), A Manuscript in the National Archives of Nepal, Kathmandu, Published in *Ancient Nepal*, No. 27, April 1974, p. 29.

opium trading activities, because in spite of the full cooperation of the Chinese officials on this occasion, this 1886 Nepalese mission also took nearly five years to complete the journey, in contrast to eighteen months, which had been normal duration prior to 1852. The Nepalese sources clearly indicate that the 1886 Nepalese mission was indeed involved in opium trading in China, for according to the Nepalese government's instructions to the leader of the Nepalese mission to China dated 11 September 1886, it seemed that the mission's members were also allowed to take some opium for their own trading purposes, but that they were strictly warned to sell the opium belonging to the ruling family first. If any member of the mission tried to sell his own article (opium) while neglecting the goods (opium) belonging to the ruling family, he was to be fined by the leader of the mission on the spot. However, if the leader of the mission was involved in such activities, he was to be fined by the Nepalese government upon his return to Nepal[23]. Thus it seemed quite clear that not only the Rana rulers but also the members of the Nepalese mission themselves were engaged in opium trading in China. It was also reported that just like the 1866 Nepalese mission, the Nepalese mission of 1886 also could not dispose of the narcotics, because the opium carried by the 1886 mission to Peking proved to be of inferior quality. *Kazi* Ran Bikram Rana, the leader of the 1886 mission, reported to *Maharaja* Bir Shamsher that no Chinese were willing to buy the Nepalese opium, for it had lost its flavour and its stickiness[24].

The next Nepalese mission was sent to China in 1894. The 1894 Nepalese mission was led by *Kazi* Major Indra Bikram Rana, a grandson of Jang Bahadur's brother Bam Bahadur[25]. Importantly enough, it was mainly due to the

---

23 Nepalese Government's instructions to the leader of the mission, dated 1943 B.S. Bhadra Sudi 13 Roj 7 (11 September 1886), MFA, Unnumbered Poka.

24 Uprety, f.n. no. 8, p. 165.

25 H. Wylie to Secretary, Govt. of India, 9 July 1894, Foreign Dept. Sec. E., July 1894, No. 184, NAI.

commercial character of this very mission, that the newspaper *The Times* dated 25 December, 1896 even referred to twenty members of 1894 Nepalese mission as traders. *The Times* further reported that those twenty delegates seemed to have taken their wares to Peking for sale[26]. It seems that it was due to its commercial nature that the mission of 1894 took nearly six and half years[27] to complete the journey, the longest time ever taken by the Nepalese mission to Peking. The Nepalese sources clearly state that, like the previous mission, this mission of 1894 too was involved in opium trading in China. Upon reading the instructions from *Maharaja* Bir Shamsher to *Kazi* Indra Bikram Rana, it seems that the 1894 mission, too, could not dispose of the opium in China[28].

Nepal sent her next customary mission to China in 1906. This happened to be the eighteenth, as well as the last Nepalese customary quinquennial mission to the Imperial court of China. The 1906 Nepalese mission was led by *Kazi* Major Bhairab Bahadur Gadhatola Chhetri[29] Like the earlier missions to China, the Nepalese court again sent opium with the 1906 mission to be sold in China. This fact is evident in a letter dated 17 August, 1907 from Tarchindeo in which the Nepalese envoy Bhairab Bahadur informed the Nepalese Prime Minister Chandra Shamsher that the opium which he had taken with him for sale on government account had not yet been sold and believed that the opium would have no sale in the open market

26 Adrian Sever, *Nepal Under the Ranas,* New Delhi: Oxford and IBH Publishing Co. Pvt. Ltd., 1993, p. 205.

27 Resident in Nepal to Secretary, Govt. of India, 15 March 1901, Foreign Dept. External B, April 1901, No. 31, NAI. But Manandhar and Mishra have wrongly stated that the 1894 Nepalese mission returned home after the lapse of seven years. See Tri Ratna Manandhar and Tirtha Prasad Mishra, *Nepal's Quinquennial Missions to China,* Kathmandu: Purna Devi Manandhar and Puspa Mishra, 1986, p. 40. Similarly Sever has wrongly stated that the 1894 Nepalese mission returned home after an absence of six years. See Sever, f.n. no. 5, pp. 167-170.

28 Uprety, f.n. no. 8, p. 165.

29 J. Manners Smith to Secretary, Govt. of India, 17 August 1906, Foreign Dept. Sec. E, September 1906, No. 263, NAI.

due to the Chinese government's policies of closing the smoking dens, the gradual restrictions on the use of opium among the people, and the gradual elimination of the cultivation of opium in the country. He had also stated that in case of the impossibility of disposing of the opium stock by any means, then he would be obliged to take the opium back again to Nepal. In the letter, *Kazi* Bhairab Bahadur also mentioned that with regard to opium, the government of China was making strenuous efforts to reduce or totally stop its use among the people, and with that view an imperial edict was issued and those who transgressed the order punished. The Nepalese envoy went on to state that he had heard that the Chinese government had started a commission to enquire and find the actual areas in which opium was cultivated, and had made an estimate of the loss to be incurred by the government upon stopping its cultivation. A final decision would be made when the commission submitted its report, but it seemed as if the cultivation of the drug was totally stopped in China by then. Due to the issuance of the order prohibiting the use of opium there at that time, very few people took opium, and those who took it, did so in secret. The Chinese opium was sold very cheaply and it appeared that the import of foreign opium had been stopped[30]. Here it should be mentioned that the first practical step towards the suppression of opium in China had been taken by the Imperial government in 1906, when it adopted a policy of taxing domestic opium out of existence. This was followed almost immediately by a policy designed to stop both the cultivation and use of opium by gradual prohibition. By 1907, encouraging progress had been achieved. In this regard it is interesting to note that an American Professor named Henry Endemenilt had met the Nepalese mission of 1906 in Bathang *enroute* to Peking and, believing the Nepalese mission to be carrying opium for sale in China, the American Professor informed *Kazi* Bhairab Bahadur about the recent Chinese edict

30 Translation of information received from *Kazi* Bhyrab Bahadur, 17 August 1907, Foreign Dept. Sec. E, March 1908, No.1, NAI.

prohibiting the use of opium by Chinese government servants and the public, the former within six months and the latter within one year, and thus the diminishing consumption of opium. The American Professor also stated that Chinese government servants did not touch it and it seemed that China would improve much in seven or eight years[31]. As stated by the American Professor, the Nepalese mission faced the problem of disposing of the opium in China. This was evident in a letter dated 11 February 1908 from Singafu (Sinhafu), in which the Nepalese envoy informed Prime Minister Chandra Shamsher that he had not yet been able to sell the opium. In the letter, the *Kazi* also mentioned that in spite of having attempted to sell the opium secretly, the opium had not yet been sold, but he stated that he would try his best to sell the opium on the way to Peking as well as in Peking[32]. While in Peking, in a conversation with Sir J.N. Jordan, the British Minister at Peking on 4 June, 1908, *Kazi* Bhairab Bahadur stated that the question of continuing the customary Nepalese mission to China appeared to him to be of doubtful utility. Former missions had been largely in the nature of commercial speculations and had proved very successful in that respect. Little profit was then to be made by bringing Nepalese produce to China. The change, although the envoy did not say so, was probably due to the restrictions placed upon the sale of opium which was, the British Minister believed, in former years one of the articles in which the Nepalese mission traded[33]. As predicted by the Nepalese envoy, the system of sending five-yearly mission to China was soon terminated by Nepal mainly on account of the new Chinese law restricting the

---

31 J. Manners Smith to Assistant Secretary, Govt. of India, 7 August 1907, Foreign Dept. Sec. E, September 1907, No. 98, NAI.

32 Bhairab Bahadur's Letter sent from Singafu, 1964 B.S. Magh 29 Roj 3 (11 February 1908), See Jnanmani Nepal, *Nepal-Bhot Chin Sambandha Ka Kehi Sanskritik Paksha* (Some Cultural Aspects of Nepal-Tibet China Relations), Kathmandu: Royal Nepal Academy, 2045 B.S., pp. 446-449.

33 J.N. Jordan to Edward Grey, 5 June 1908, Foreign Dept. Sec. E, October 1908, No. 709, NAI.

sale of opium in China. It was not known how much opium the 1906 Nepalese mission carried to China for sales purpose; but it seems that the mission could not dispose of the opium which it had carried to Peking, because, from the Chinese capital also, the Nepalese *Kazi* informed the Nepalese Premier that due to the strict implementation of anti-opium regulations in China, the opium, which the Nepalese mission had carried, had not yet been sold[34]. While returning from Peking, the Nepalese mission met the *Chundu* (governor) of Paochinfu in Tientsin. It was reported that the *Chundu* of Paochinfu had stated that if the Nepalese envoy brought back with him a lot of things which could not be sold at Peking, then he (the *Chundu*) promised to help the Nepalese envoy dispose of the things. At that time, the Nepalese *Kazi* told the *Chundu* of Paochinfu that he had brought only a small quantity of things, and that as the unsold things were few in quantity, he was taking them back with him[35]. But one Nepalese source states that the *Chundu* of Paochinfu helped the Nepalese mission to dispose all the unsold goods[36].

Importantly enough the Rana rulers were well aware of the fact that opium was an "irrepressible drug" and that the Chinese as well as the Tibetans indulged in opium smoking. Besides that, they also knew that opium was not only in great demand in China but that it was sold at a high price in China. The opium trade in China become of even greater importance at the time of Prime Minister Jang Bahadur. An official note from the British Minister at Peking in 1876 clearly mentioned that through the so-called embassy, Prime Minister Jang Bahadur managed every five years to land a considerable cargo of opium in the western provinces of China without paying the heavy maritime duty and "lekin" taxes. The high price of opium and its

34 *Kazi* Bhairab Bahadur's letter, 1965 B.S. Baisakh 24 Gate Roj 3 (April 1908), MFA Poka No. 64, Ka 51.

35 Translation of *Kazi* Bhairab Bahadur's letter, 15 September 1908, Foreign Dept. January 1909, No. 413, NAI.

36 Nepal, f.n. no. 32, p. 374.

shortage for internal consumption, including the low price paid to the ryots, encouraged the growth of opium in the Tarai areas of Nepal, where it was regulated by the government and the produce was bought from the ryots[37]. Furthermore it also prompted the illegal opium trade in China. It seems that so long as the five-yearly missions to China were maintained, the Nepalese government took advantage of that opening to introduce a large quantity of opium into China by the overland route under the auspices of its Envoy. Here it should be mentioned that the growth of opium was then compulsory for Nepalese ryots, who were also forced to sell it to the agents of the Nepalese court at rates which they considered to be unremunerative. But afterwards, the government monopoly on opium was abolished; and so the Nepalese ryots had an unrestricted right to cultivate opium and sell it to whom they pleased, including the opium agents of the British government[38]. Due to this, there were no inducements to smuggle opium into British territory. But there were the reports of alleged illicit traffic in opium through Nepal[39]. From the above account it becomes evident that the Rana's had encouraged the growth of opium in the Tarai areas of Nepal and profited a lot by sending a large quantities of opium along with the Nepalese mission for sale in China.

Interestingly enough, the Nepalese *Vakil* at Lhasa was also involved in matters relating to the opium trade. Whenever the Nepalese missions to China could not sell the whole stock of opium in China, they used to bring back the remaining portion of opium to Lhasa. In that event the Nepalese *Vakil* was bound to sell it at the markets of Lhasa. The Nepalese documents indicate that at one time, Jang Bahadur authorised the Nepalese

---

37 Daniel Wright, Officiating Resident in Nepal to Secretary, Govt. of India, 27 February 1875, Foreign Polt. A, May 1875, No. 104, NAI.

38 Girdlestone to Secretary, Govt. of India, 26 June 1873, Foreign Polt. A, May 1875, No. 104A, NAI.

39 Alleged Illicit traffic in opium through Nipal. Foreign Polt A, May 1875, Nos. 104-104A, NAI.

Vakil at Lhasa to employ six *Siphais* (soldiers) to guard the large quantity of opium deposited in the *Vakil's* office, and an annual amount of rupees two hundred and eighty eight was sanctioned to pay the *Siphais*. Thus the Nepalese *Vakil* at Lhasa had to work as an agent of the opium trade initiated by Nepalese Prime Minister[40]. The ruling Rana family of Nepal, especially the Rana Prime Minister and the Commander-in-Chief, exported contraband goods like opium through the Nepalese quinquennial missions and the Nepalese merchants in order to sell them at Lhasa. It was reported that in 1873 a consignment of opium in which the Nepalese court was interested, valued at rupees fifty thousand was stopped at the border by the Tibetans[41]. The Nepalese documents state that the Nepalese *Vakil* at Lhasa used to get some money if he succeeded in selling a sufficient quantity of opium belonging to the ruling Rana family. If not, it was likely that he would even be dismissed. Several contemporary records indicate that the Prime Minister was greatly annoyed if the Nepalese *Vakil* at Lhasa could not sell the opium for a sufficient profit[42]. All the more, one Nepalese document dated 1921 B.S. Baisak Badi 13 Roj 4 (April 1864) reveals that once even the Chinese *Amban* had sent one person to Captain Chandraman Karki Chhetri, the Nepalese *Vakil* at Lhasa requesting him to make available a good quality of opium[43]. This clearly evidenced that the Nepalese *Vakil* worked as an agent of the opium trade in Lhasa.

Here it should be also mentioned that initially, that is, in the pre-Rana period, the Nepalese missions normally took a year and half to cover the journey both ways, especially after the rise of the Ranas, when the five-yearly missions changed their character from political to commercial, and the duration of these

---

40 Tri Ratna Manandhar, *Some Aspects of Rana Rule in Nepal*, Kathmandu: Purna Devi Manandhar, 1983, pp. 22-23.

41 Jahar Sen, *Indo-Nepal Trade in the Nineteenth Century*, Calcutta: Firma KLM Pvt. Ltd., 1977, p. 121.

42 Manandhar, f.n. no. 40, p. 22.

43 Nepal, f.n. no. 32, p. 445.

Nepalese missions to China became much longer. Both the 1877 and 1886 Nepalese missions to Peking returned home after an absence of five years, whereas the 1894 and 1906 missions took six and half years and four years respectively. The longer duration of these missions were mainly due to their commercial activities, particularly opium trade. As the ruling Rana family was involved in the illegal trade of opium through these mission members, the Nepalese missions had to stay in Chinese territory for a long period to sell opium and other goods as directed by the ruling family. Likewise, as to the duration of the sojurn of the Nepalese mission at Peking, in the pre-Rana period the Nepalese missions generally remained at Peking for forty five days. But in the Rana period, due to their involvement in trading activities, especially the opium trade, the Nepalese missions started staying at Peking for a longer period, for the 1877 Nepalese mission led by *Kazi* Tej Bahadur Rana remained at Peking for more than five months[44]. Similarly, the 1906 Nepalese mission led by *Kazi* Bhairab Bahadur remained in the Chinese capital for five months[45].

The mission system was profitable financially not only for the Nepalese rulers, but for the members of the mission as well, so there were reports that senior Nepalese officers competed keenly to be selected to lead the missions[46], for they enjoyed an exemption from all customs duties on both the

---

44 T.F. Wade, Her Majesty's Minister at Peking to Viceroy of India, 16 January 1880, Foreign Dept. Polt. A., April 1880, No. 98, NAI. and Her Majesty's Minister at Peking to Ripon, Viceroy of India, 1 November 1880, Foreign Polt. A, January 1881, No. 84, NAI.

45 J.N. Jordan to Edward Grey, 29 April 1908, Foreign Dept. Sec. E, October 1908, No. 705, NAI. and J.N. Jordan to Edward Grey, 14 September 1908, Foreign Dept. Sec. E, January 1909, No. 411, NAI.

46 C.W. Ravenshaw, Resident in Nepal to Secretary, Govt. of India, 28 June 1902, Foreign Sec. E, September 1902, Nos. 127-133, NAI. Prime Minister Chandra Shamsher himself had told J.Manners Smith, the British Resident in Nepal that the *Kazi* who led the Nepalese mission to Peking got one *lakh* rupees and other members also got similar monetary benefits. See, Manandhar and Mishra, f.n. no. 27, p. 71.

outwards and return journeys, and the profits to be made on the goods that they carried, especially opium, were staggering. Likewise, from the commercial activities of the mission, particularly due to opium trading in China, the Nepalese rulers benefited greatly. Thus the prospect of profitable commercial transactions through the opium trade had motivated the Rana rulers to send periodical missions to China until 1906 despite all sorts of humiliations and obstacles created by the Chinese authorities. While writing a letter dated 19 April 1906 to Major J.Manners Smith, the officiating British Resident in Nepal, Prime Minister Chandra Shamsher clearly stated the commercial nature of the Nepalese quinquennial mission to China in the following words: "They are merely a means for the party to gain access into the country under very advantageous circumstances, and to dispose of with very great profit the large sum of goods which they take with them. It may be known to you, that all goods belonging to the party are carried free from our frontier to Peking and back by the transport provided by the Chinese government, which also provides our men, free, with all necessaries on the road. It has very little political significance....."[47]. But once the Chinese government made strict rules imposing restrictions on the sale of prohibited goods like opium, the Nepalese mission indeed suffered a great monetary loss. That is why *Kazi* Bhairab Bahadur had doubted the utility of continuing the Nepalese quinquennial mission to Peking after 1906. As he predicted, the system of sending Nepalese five-yearly missions to China was soon terminated by Nepal mainly on account of the new Chinese law restricting the sale of opium in China.

Thus we see that with the appearance of the Ranas on the political scene in Nepal, especially with the mission of 1852, the purpose of the Nepalese mission to China became more commercial for the personal profit of the Rana Prime Minister

---

47 Chandra Shamsher to J.Manners Smith, Officiating Resident in Nepal, 19 April 1906, Foreign Dept. Sec. E, June 1906, No. 243, NAI.

and his close relatives than for national interest. From 1852 to 1906, all six Nepalese missions to China were engaged in the opium trade. As such, it would not be improper to refer to them as commercial or trading missions to China. Due to the changing nature of the Nepalese mission from political to commercial, Indian Archival documents have often referred to those missions even in the headings of the Foreign Department records as "Nepalese Commercial Missions to China". Thus the Nepalese quinquennial missions to China ceased to have any political significance and assumed the character of lucrative trading ventures for the personal benefit of the rulers. It is beyond doubt that the Nepalese missions' involvement in the opium trade in China was indeed a misuse of the diplomatic mission for the personal pecuniary benefit of Rana Prime Ministers and their brothers. It is strong evidence of how the Ranas misused diplomatic relations between the two countries. The Ranas' lust for wealth could not be satisfied by the exploitation of national resources only, so the Ranas compelled the officials to smuggle contraband goods like opium to China, sometimes even females to sell.

***

China's Enlistment of People of Mixed Nepalese-Tibetan Ancestry*

Till now, almost all the writers are of the view that China did not enlist Nepalese-Tibetans for her military service, but this is not true. The Indian National Archival documents shed some new light on this matter. As such, according to the Indian Archival documents, an attempt is made in this brief paper to discuss China's enlistment of the Nepalese-Tibetans for her military service.

Following Younghusband's withdrawal from Lhasa in September, 1904, China attempted to reassert its authority over Tibet. For that purpose, she took several measures, such as dispatching to Tibet a powerful "Special Commissioner", Chang Yin-t'ang, and the thorough reorganization of the Tibetan administration. She also followed the policy of increasing the number of Chinese troops in Tibet, particularly in Lhasa. Meanwhile Chinese *Amban(*Resident*)*-Lien-Yu and General Chang Yin-t'ang tried to keep the Nepalese *Vakil*(envoy) at Lhasa, Major Captain Jit Bahadur Khatri Chhetri, in good humour. The Chinese *Amban* informed the Nepalese *Vakil* about the increasing number of Chinese troops in Tibet and also hinted about his intention to enlist Nepalese soldiers[1]. Similarly, General Chang Yin-t'ang also asked the Nepalese *Vakil* about the possibility of obtaining Nepalese soldiers for the *Amban's*

---

* Published in *Rolamba*, Vol. 16, No. 1 (January-March 1996), pp. 7-10.

1 Translation of a letter from the Nepalese representative at Lhasa, 13 December 1906, Foreign Secret E, May 1907, No. 212, National Archives of India (NAI), New Delhi.

guards at Lhasa. But the Chinese proposal was rejected by the Nepalese government[2]. In the meantime the Chinese *Amban* succeeded in recruiting one hundred Tibetans for the Chinese army[3]. It was said that many men of bad character from Lhasa were included amongst the newly recruited soldiers[4]. It was also reported that Tang Tarin *Amban* had appointed forty to fifty soldiers from amongst the people of mixed Chinese and Tibetan ancestry[5].

Here it should be mentioned that according to one source, there were over a thousand persons of mixed Nepalese and Tibetan parentage (referred to as *Khachadas*) in Lhasa alone[6]. A large number of *Khachada* traders also lived in Shigatse and other southern Tibetan cities and villages. They generally dressed, lived and worshipped as the Tibetans did. Meanwhile, due to the increasingly strained relations between the Chinese *Amban* and the *Kasyal* office and the feeling of insecurity in Lhasa, the Chinese *Amban* asked the Nepalese government to permit three hundred Nepalese-Tibetans to be enlisted in the Chinese army. But the Nepalese government flatly refused to give such permission. Nepal even forbade the voluntary enlistment of Nepalese-Tibetans into the Chinese military service[7]. The Nepalese *Vakil* told the Chinese *Amban* that they were very unsuited for military service. In spite of that, the Chinese enlisted nine Nepalese-Tibetans for their military service. The Nepalese *Vakil*, Jit Bahadur reported to the

---

2 Leo E. Rose, *Nepal: Strategy For Survival,* Berkeley: University of California Press, 1971, p. 162.

3 Translation of *Kazi Bhairab Bahadur's letter*, 18 January 1907, Foreign Secret E, June 1907, No. 86, NAI.

4 Translation of a letter from the Nepalese representative at Lhasa, 31 January 1907, Foreign Secret E, June 1907, No. 88, NAI.

5 Translation of a letter from the Nepalese representative at Lhasa, 18 January 1907, Foreign Secret E, June 1907, No. 87, NAI.

6 Charles Bell, *Tibet: Past and Present,* Delhi: Motilal Banarsidass Publishers Pvt. Ltd., Reprint, 1992, p. 233.

7 Francis Tuker, *Gorkha: The Story of the Gurkhas of Nepal,* London: Constable and Company Ltd., 1957, p. 190.

Nepalese Prime Minister Chandra Shamsher that the Chinese local authorities made great efforts to enlist recruits for their troops from the Chinese, Tibetan, Nepalese mixed race population and Muslims, without discrimination. None who had a means of livelihood cared to accept this service when it was offered to them[8]. According to the Nepalese *Vakil's* reports, the Chinese managed to get hold of some low class Tibetans and beggars and the Tibetan government was thinking of protesting against that practice, and that when the said government was ready to supply the Chinese authorities, they could have availed of the offer. In a letter dated 5 October 1909, to Lieutenant-Colonel J. Manners Smith, British Resident in Nepal, the Nepalese Prime Minister Chandra Shamsher mentioned the Nepalese *Vakil's* letter regarding China's enlistment of nine Nepalese-Tibetans for her military service[9]. The Nepalese *Vakil* Jit Bahadur had already informed the Nepalese Premier that all of the nine enlisted Nepalese-Tibetans were either beggars or bad characters with no ostensible means of livelihood. The Nepalese *Vakil's* furnishing of the list of the Nepalese-Tibetans who were enlisted by the Chinese for their military service were as follows:

1. Hundu, the son of a beggar named Lubhu *Khachada* (mixed race), used to do a little work making "Docha" (Tibetan shoes) and had nothing to live upon.

2. Chhongay Losang, who formerly used to do a little work making "Docha", had no ostensible means of livelihood.

3. Hadi, who formerly used to do a little smith's work, had no ostensible means of livelihood. A brother of Thuten Norbu *Khachada*.

---

8 Chandra Shamsher to J. Manners-Smith, 5 October 1909, Foreign Secret E, October 1909, No. 716, NAI.

9 *Ibid.*

4. Tenda, had no ostensible means of livelihood, and another brother of Thuten Norbu.

5. Baboo, who had no home or ostensible means of livelihood. A brother of Wonju *Khachada*.

6. Dhoka Wonju, had no home or ostensible means of livelihood.

7. Jhowa Chhiring, formerly used to do a little work selling drugs or medicine, but had no ostensible means of livelihood.

8. Dhundu, a homeless beggar.

9. Sango, a homeless beggar used to go about begging, singing and dancing[10].

In this way, the Nepalese *Vakil* Jit Bahadur's letter to Prime Minister Chandra Shamsher clearly mentioned about the enlistment of nine Nepalese-Tibetans by China for her military service. Thus it disproves the earlier assumption of China not enlisting Nepalese-Tibetans. However, it should not be forgotten that despite the Nepalese government's having forbidden the voluntary enlistment of Nepalese-Tibetans, the Chinese not only manipulated but also succeeded in enlisting nine Nepalese-Tibetans for their military service.

***

10 *Ibid.*

China's Recruitment of Ex-Gurkha Soldiers: A Peep into the Forgotten Past*

We have heard a lot about the Nepalese youths employed in the British army, but we have not heard of China's employment of ex-Gurkha (Nepalese) soldiers of the British Gorkha army as instructors in her army. Some documents from the National Archives of India shed some new light on this topic. Based upon those documents, an attempt is made here to discuss the employment of ex-Gurkha soldiers of the British Gorkha army as drill instructors in the Chinese army.

Here it will not be out of context to briefly mention the coming of the Gurkhas to Burma. The arrival of the Gurkhas in Burma started with the third Anglo-Burmese war of 1885-1886, in which the Gurkhas played an important role. This very war resulted in the British occupation of Burma which became politically and administratively a part of British India in 1886. From 1897 to 1923, Burma was placed under a Lieutenant-Governor. Soon after Burma was incorporated into the British Empire, two more regiments of Gurkhas, i.e., 7th and 10th Gurkha rifles were raised there. These two regiments were raised mainly from the Burma Military Police battalions, for at that time the Gurkhas were coming down from the hills to enlist in the police as well as in the army. The 10th Gurkha rifles

---

* Published in *Voice of History*, Vol. XII, No. 1 (July 1997), pp. 61-66.

remained in Burma at its home in Maymyo, a beautiful spot in the Shan hills to the east of Mandalay[1].

According to the notes in the General Staff Branch of India[2], the Commander-in-Chief of the British Indian army heard from Major–General Sir R. Scallon, Commander of the Burma Division, that the Chinese were taking Gurkhas who had left British Indian army as instructors for their troops. The General Staff Branch of India had some information that natives of India–Gurkhas, and others as well–frequently cut their names or deserted from the Military Police Battalions of Burma near the Chinese frontier, and settled down in the Chinese province of Yunnan after marrying local women. In Yunnan, they generally made a living as milksellers, and so forth, and had, in most instances, no intention of returning to their own country. According to the information received by the General Staff Branch of India, as yet the Gurkhas did not appear to have been utilised by the Chinese for the purpose of instructing their troops. The General Staff Branch felt that it was not easy to devise means for preventing the Gurkhas from putting their military knowledge at the disposal of their potential enemy, since it had practically no hold over those people once they were out of British territory. The General Staff Branch thought that the Foreign Department of India may perhaps be able to say whether it would be possible, through the British Consuls in China, to bring some influence to bear on such men trained by the British, threatening them and their families with life-long banishment from British India should they persist in following a course so opposed to British interests near the British borders. The General Staff Branch firmly believed that any action by the Foreign Department that might be conceived would help put an end to such an undesirable state of affairs. The British Indian government could not remain aloof from this sensitive issue. As

---

1 Duncan Forbes, *Johnny Gurkha*, London: Robert Hale, 1964, pp. 85-86

2 Notes in the General Staff Branch, 8 June 1911, Foreign External B, September 1911, No. 94, National Archives of India (NAI), New Delhi.

such, Mr. E.H.S. Clarke, Deputy Secretary to the government of India in the Foreign Department, enquired with Mr. Rose, the British Consul at Tengyueh, China about this topic[3]. Mr. Rose told Mr. Clarke that in his long experience in Yunnan and the frontier country, he had never seen a single case of an ex-British Gurkha soldier residing there. Mr. Rose also stated that the Chinese, as a rule, did not use milk, and it was unlikely that there would be any market for milk-vendors, except possibly at Yunnan-fu, or on the Tonkin border. He went on to say that he had never seen or received any information of a Gurkha employed in drilling Chinese troops. Mr. Rose was very doubtful if it would be possible to proceed against any Gurkha who might cross the border, but he thought it might be advisable to inform the British Consuls in Yunnan of any specific case which would come to the notice of the military authorities, and they would certainly take any step within their power to safeguard British military interests.

Meanwhile the Commanding Officer of the 10th Gurkha Rifle at Maymyo, Burma, reported to the General Staff Branch of India about the following specific cases as such:

a. *Naik* Man Bahadur Limbu, who deserted from the 10th Gurkhas in the year 1910, was now an instructor for the Chinese troops in Yunnan.

b. *Naik* Asbir Rai, formerly in the 10th Gurkhas, took his discharge, and was now in the Chinese service in Yunnan. Two or three other Gurkhas also went with him[4].

---

3 Notes in the Foreign Department, 24 June 1911, Foreign External B, September 1911, No. 94, NAI.

4 E.H.S. Clarke, Deputy Secretary to the Government of India in the Foreign Department to H. Thompson, Officiating Chief Secretary to the Government of Burma, 3 July 1911, Foreign External B, September 1911, No. 94. NAI

After receiving the aforementioned information on 3 July, 1911, Mr. E.H.S. Clarke, Deputy Secretary to the Government of India in the Foreign Department, informed Mr. H. Thompson, Officiating Chief Secretary to the government of Burma, Rangoon, regarding the specific cases of ex-Gurkha soldiers of the British Indian army entering the Chinese military service in Yunnan as reported by the Commanding Officer of the 10th Gurkhas at Maymyo[5]. Mr. Clarke stated that it was doubtful whether it would be possible to take official cognisance of such cases, but he believed that British Consular Officers might be able to discourage their employment by the Chinese. With this view in mind, Mr. Clarke requested to Mr. Thompson that if the Lieutenant-Governor of Burma saw no objection, then the matter might be brought to the notice of the British Consul at Tengyueh and the British Consul-General at Yunnan-fu, and that they might be asked to take such steps as might be possible or expedient to safeguard British military interests. On 18 July, 1911, Mr. Thompson informed Mr. Clarke that in accordance with the wishes of the government of India, the government of Burma had asked both the British Consul - General at Yunnan-fu and the British Consul at Tengyueh to make enquiries about the ex-Gurkha soldiers of the British Indian army who entered the Chinese military service in Yunnan[6]. On 5 October, 1911, Mr. Thompson dispatched to Mr. Clarke a copy of a letter, dated 28 August, 1911, from Mr. P.E.O'Brien-Butler, the British Consul-General for Yunnan and Kueichou regarding the employment of Gurkhas as instructors for Chinese troops in Yunnan after they had left the British Indian army[7]. In the letter, Mr. Butler stated that he found an opportunity to talk with the Chinese Commissioner of Foreign Affairs, mentioning the subject of the employment of ex-Gurkha soldiers as instructors

5 *Ibid.*

6 H. Thompson to E.H.S. Clarke, 18 July 1911, Foreign External B, September 1911, No. 94, NAI.

7 H. Thompson to E.H.S. Clarke, 5 October 1911, Foreign External B, January 1912, No. 730, NAI.

to Chinese troops in Yunnan. Mr. Butler tried his best to convince the Chinese Commissioner of Foreign Affairs that from the British government's point of view, the employment of such persons was undesirable. Mr. Butler succeeded better in persuading the Chinese Commissioner that their military knowledge was after all extremely limited[8]. The Chinese Commissioner told Mr. Butler that he had never heard of Indian ex-soldiers being employed in the Yunnan army in any capacity whatsoever, and he doubted strongly if any were in fact employed. He promised, however, to make careful enquiries and let the British Consul-General know the results as soon as possible.

According to the notes in Foreign Department of India dated 1 July, 1911, after receiving information regarding specific cases of ex-Gurkha soldiers of the British Indian army entering the Chinese military service in Yunnan as reported by the Commanding Officer of the 10th Gurkhas at Maymyo, Mr. Arthur Henry Mc Mohan, Secretary of State of the Government of India, decided to ask the British Resident in Nepal whether or not it would be possible to bring such pressures to bear on the offenders' families in Nepal as would deter Gurkhas from such practice[9]. Mr. Mc Mohan opined that that would of course only be necessary in the case of those who entered the Chinese military service as instructors or otherwise. Accordingly, on 6 July, 1911, Mr. E.H.S. Clarke, Deputy Secretary to the government of India in the Foreign Department, informed Lieutenant-Colonel J. Manners-Smith, the British Resident in Nepal, regarding recent cases of ex-Gurkha soldiers of the British Indian army entering the Chinese military service in Yunnan. Mr. Clarke also asked Lieutenant-Colonel Smith to enquire whether it would be possible for the Nepalese court to

---

8 P.E.O'Brien Butler, British Consul–General for Yunnan and Kueichou to Thompson, Foreign External B, January 1912, No. 730, NAI.

9 Notes in the Foreign Department, 1 July 1911, Foreign External B, September 1911, No. 94, NAI.

assist, by bringing such pressure to bear on the families of the men concerned, as would tend to deter Gurkhas from such practice, which was seriously opposed to British interests as well as those of Nepal, a fact which the Nepalese Prime Minister would doubtless at once recognise. On 16 August, 1911, the British Resident in Nepal reported to Mr. Clarke that before making any reference to the Nepalese Court, he wrote confidentially to the Officer Commanding the 1st - 10th Gurkhas asking for the home addresses in Nepal of the two Gurkhas said to have taken service with the Chinese in Yunnan. The Commanding Officer of the 1st - 10th Gurkhas was able to send the home address in Nepal of *Naik* Man Bahadur Limbu, but not of *Naik* Asbir Rai, who was transferred to the 2nd battalion in September 1908. As such, the British Resident asked the Commanding Officer of the 2nd - 10th Gurkhas for the home address in Nepal of *Naik* Asbir Rai[10]. The British Resident also stated that he took the opportunity to speak to the Nepalese Prime Minister Chandra Shamsher on the subject of Gurkhas entering service under the Chinese. The Nepalese Premier told the British Resident that he had heard nothing about that matter, but that he would be very sorry if such a practice should arise. In the letter, the British Resident reminded Mr. Clarke that the Nepalese Prime Minister was careful to reject all applications for the recruitment of Gurkhas and even of the Nepalese-Tibetans in Lhasa for the service of the Tibetan government and the Chinese. According to Lieutenant-Colonel Smith, the Nepalese Prime Minister told him that as regards a means of restricting such new development, he would be ready to make it a rule that the Gurkhas who entered the service abroad under the Chinese government should be refused *Pani Patiya* or re-admission to caste privileges on return to Nepal, and that he would also deal with individual cases when reported to him. The

---

10 Lieutenant-Colonel J. Manners–Smith, Resident in Nepal to E.H.S. Clarke, Deputy Secretary to the government of India in the Foreign Department, 16 August 1911, Foreign External B, September 1911, No 94, NAI.

British Resident then informed the Nepalese Prime Minister in writing of the two cases which had been brought to the attention of the government of India, and gave him the address in Nepal of *Naik* Man Bahadur Limbu[11].

The aforementioned discussion made it clear that there were two reported specific cases of ex-Gurkha soldiers of the British Indian army entering the Chinese military service in Yunnan. Although both the Chinese Commissioner of Foreign Affairs and the Nepalese Prime Minister Chandra Shamsher denied any knowledge about those reported specific cases, just on the basis of their denial alone, we cannot say that the two reported specific cases were baseless. Due to the proximity of Yunnan to the Chinese border from Burma, there was a great possibility that such cases could occur. Under such circumstances, there is no room for doubt about those reported specific cases. Otherwise, the Commanding Officer of the 10th Gurkhas at Maymyo would not have reported them. Here it should be also mentioned that in spite of the Nepalese government's having forbidden even the voluntary enlistment of the Nepalese-Tibetans into the Chinese military service, the Chinese succeeded in enlisting nine Nepalese-Tibetans for their troops in 1909[12]. Meanwhile, we must not forget that the aforementioned subject is mentioned only in Indian Archival documents. So far, no indigeneous document has been detected up to this time to shed more light on this subject. There is no doubt that only after closely examining the Nepalese documents, can we have a detailed and correct view about this subject. It is a pity that Nepal has very scanty information on many events, as such on this subject also we have no information. Moreover, the subject did not draw any attention, as the number of Nepalese joining the Chinese army was very, very negligible and

11 *Ibid.*

12 *Maharaja* Chandra Shamsher to Lieutenant-Colonel J. Manners-Smith, British Resident in Nepal, 5 October 1909, Foreign Secret E, October 1909, No. 716, NAI.

their role in the Chinese army seemed to be very minor. It was like a drop of water in the ocean. Thus, the matter remained ignored in the annals of the history. However, just based on the silence of the existing Nepalese documents alone, it would not be fair to challenge the authenticity of the aforementioned specific cases of ex-Gurkha soldiers of the British Indian army entering the Chinese military service in Yunnan.

Moreover the Britishers' concern of a Nepali joining any service of any country is also a matter to be taken into consideration. A citizen of a sovereign independent country can join service anywhere in the world so long it does not go against the national interest of the mother country. It was a high handedness of the Britishers' over a small country like Nepal.

***

The Chinese Missions of 1930 and 1932 to Nepal*

After the Nepal-Tibet-China war of 1788-1792, a new relationship was established between Nepal and China through the sending of Nepalese missions to China every five years. This new trend in Sino-Nepalese relations continued until 1906. Afterwards it was mainly due to China's claim of Suzerainty over Nepal in 1910 that the Nepalese five-yearly trading missions did not turn out to be profitable due to China's having put certain restrictions upon them, and the Chinese Revolution of 1911 which resulted in the overthrow of the Ch'ing dynasty and the establishment of the Republic of China under Dr. Sun Yat-Sen, that the Nepalese government terminated over a century old mission system by not dispatching the customary Nepalese quinquennial mission to China in 1911. Even then, through intrigues China made futile attempts to bring Nepal under her influence. From that period onwards, Nepal became more and more aloof toward China. In this way, from 1914 to 1955, Nepal showed no inclination to maintain relations with China except through the sending of one lone Nepalese goodwill mission to China in April 1947. During that period relations with China were limited to the reception of four Chinese missions to Kathmandu, mainly sent to confer titles and to present ceremonial robes to the Rana Prime Ministers of Nepal. Thus we see that due to the Kaleidoscopic changes in the political situation in China since the establishment of the Republic which was followed by the complete lack of a responsible government, a complete rupture of relations between Nepal and China ensued, even though they were not officially

---

* Published in *Rolamba*, Vol. 16, No. 3 (July-September 1996), pp. 12-14.

severed. Despite that, the Nationalist government of China made a few feeble attempts to re-establish contacts with the Nepalese government in the period from 1930 to 1946 by dispatching four missions to Nepal in 1930, 1932, 1934 and 1946. Regarding those four Chinese missions, not much is known about them. The Chinese sources which are still not so used much by writers and historians shed some new light on this matter. As such, on the basis of those Chinese sources as well as other available Nepalese and Western sources, an attempt is made in this brief paper to discuss the Chinese missions of 1930 and 1932 to Nepal.

The Chinese Mission of 1930 to Nepal

Here it should be mentioned that the break in relations between Nepal and China since the establishment of a Republic in China was due to the lack of a responsible government in China. The Chinese government was fully occupied by the troubles at home, for the establishment of the Chinese Republic was soon followed by a period of Warlords when interminable civil war made China not much more than a geographical expression, like Germany in the later centuries of the Holy Roman Empire. The Warlords were succeeded by the Nationalist government of China in 1928 under Chiang Kai-Shek. Besides that there were other reasons for the rupture of Sino-Nepalese relations in the post-1912 period; the Hindu religion of Nepal forbade the Nepalese to cross the ocean due to the belief that they could not cross the ocean without losing their caste. The mission sent by Nepal to China had to take a route through Tibet. This was, however, accompanied by great hardships and even by the intentional ill-treatment by the Tibetans during their passage through Tibet. Even Nepalese Prime Minister Bhim Shamsher was reported to have stated: "Tibet has blocked our way to China"[1]. In this way, besides

1 Daniel J. Lee, "National China Re-Establishes Relations with the Kingdom of Nepal", *The China Weekly Review,* Shanghai, Vol. 55, 27 December. 1930, p. 148.

other reasons, Tibet too seemed responsible for the breaking of Sino-Nepalese relations to a large extent. Whatever the case may be, the Nationalist government of China under Chiang Kai-Shek, with a view of renewing relations with the Nepalese government, dispatched Pa Ve Sun[2], Councillor of the Committee of Mongolian and Tibetan Affairs, on a friendly mission to Nepal in May 1930. Mr. Pa was accompanied by Daniel J. Lee, who served the mission in the capacity of English Secretary[3]. The Chinese mission brought letters and various presents to the Nepalese King and the Prime Minister. Interestingly enough, at that time the letters brought by the Chinese mission were written in English, contrary to the old tradition of writing in Nepali. The Nepalese King Tribhuvan Bir Bikram Shah's and the Nepalese Prime Minister Bhim Shamsher's replies to the Chinese President Chiang Kai-Shek were written in Nepali and English language respectively[4].

After presenting their credentials to the Nepalese Prime Minister Bhim Shamsher, the Chinese delegates had several interviews with him. During the course of these interviews, they talked freely about many subjects, including political and social issues[5]. It was reported that in the letter sent through this mission to the Nepalese King Tribhuvan, the Chinese President Chiang Kai-Shek had stated: "To the end that peace and security may be maintained, the National Government (of China) will assume the responsibility to settle the boundary dispute between Nepal and Tibet"[6]. In his reply to the Chinese President Chiang Kai-Shek, the Nepalese King Tribhuvan expressed his gratitude for sending the friendly Chinese mission along with the letter

---

2 Jnanmani has referred Pa Ve Sun as Pa Wen Ching (Chin). See; Jnanmani Nepal, *Nepal-Bhot Chin Sambandha Ka Kehi Sanskritik Paksha* (Some Cultural Aspects of Nepal-Tibet-China Relations), Kathmandu: Royal Nepal Academy, 2045 B.S., p. 397 and pp. 466-467.

3 Lee, f.n. no. 1, p. 148.

4 Nepal, f.n.. no. 2, p. 397 and pp. 466-467.

5 Lee, f.n. no. 1, p. 149.

6 Michael C.Van Walt Van Praag, *The Status of Tibet*, Colorado: Westview Press, 1987, pp. 77-78.

and the presents[7]. But in his reply to the Chinese President Chiang Kai-Shek, the Nepalese Premier Bhim Shamsher "repudiated *in toto* any claim of the Chinese Government to interfere in any question of this nature"[8]. In this way, the Nepalese Prime Minister's reply served to emphasize again that China had no role whatsoever to play in Nepal-Tibet relations after 1911. Through this Chinese mission of 1930, the Nepalese Prime Minister Bhim Shamsher sent to Chinese President Chiang Kai-Shek the following presents:

1. One Tiger skin
2. One pair of Rhino horns
3. One Ivory carved box
4. Two pairs of Nepalese national weapons (*Khukuris*)
5. One set of Nepalese coins (gold, silver and copper)
6. One Carved picture frame made of wood
7. One Crystal Buddha
8. One Crystal elephant
9. A pair of brass lions
10. One brass Buddha
11. Two Suits of Nepalese dress
12. Two pieces of Nepalese golden brocade
13. A pair of Ivory spoons
14. One Wooden Carved box
15. One Ivory Knife
16. An Album with Nepalese views[9].

It was reported that the Chinese Consular-General for India, C.F. Leo provided invaluable assistance for this 1930 Chinese mission to Nepal. The Chinese mission stayed in Kathmandu for almost six weeks. The Nepalese Prime Minister Bhim Shamsher bestowed upon the Chinese mission every courtesy and generosity and ministered to their comfort and convenience as well. This Chinese mission seemed to have

7 Nepal, f.n. no. 2, pp. 466-467.
8 Van Walt Van Praag, f.n. no. 6, p. 78.
9 Lee, f.n. no. 1, p. 149.

returned to Nanking, the then Capital of China *via* India, around December 1930 after spending almost half a year abroad.

The Chinese Mission of 1932 to Nepal

In February 1932, the Chinese Nationalist government sent a special mission to Nepal for the exclusive purpose of bestowing Chinese titles upon the Nepalese Prime Minister Bhim Shamsher. This 1932 Chinese mission was dispatched to Nepal in recognition of the friendly attitude of Nepalese Prime Minister Bhim Shamsher and the goodwill of the Nepalese government towards China. The mission was headed by Chang Ming, the Chinese Consul-General in Calcutta. The Chinese Envoy Chang Ming was accompanied by his wife Mrs. Chang Ming and D.J. Lee, Special Commissioner of Mongolian and Tibetan Affairs of the National Government, who also served as Secretary to the Chinese Envoy[10].

It was reported that on 8 February, 1932, the Chinese Envoy, accompanied by his Secretary, were carried to His Majesty's former Palace Hanuman Dhoka by a four-horse drawn state carriage under the escort of Honorary General Anand Shamsher and seventeen royal Guards. Upon the Chinese Envoy's departure from the government guest house (the Chinese Envoy's temporary quarter) at 12.25 p.m., a salute of twenty one guns was fired in honour of the Chinese Envoy. When he arrived at His Majesty's Palace at Hanuman Dhoka, the Royal band played the Chinese national anthem. After the Chinese Envoy alighted from the carriage, the Nepalese Prime Minister Bhim Shamsher received the Chinese Envoy's hand in and ushered him to the farther end of the Palace by the right side of the throne. During that special official function in Kathmandu, the Chinese Envoy Chang Ming conferred on the Nepalese Prime Minister Bhim Shamsher the Honorary rank of General of the Chinese Army with the title of *Luh Chuan Shang Chiang* and the Order of *Yet Tens Pao-ting Shun Chen* First

---

10 Daniel J. Lee, "The Prime Minister of Nepal Decorated By China", *The China Weekly Review*, Shanghai, Vol. 60, 9 April, 1932, p. 188.

Class (Land, Naval and Air Force decorations), both of which were the highest honours of the Chinese Government[11].

A few days after the investiture ceremony of 8 February 1932, another special function was organised in Kathmandu in which the Nepalese government conferred on the Chinese Envoy Chang Ming the most "Refulgent of the 2nd Class Star of Nepal" (*Nepal Tara*). In this way Chang Ming became possibly the first Chinese official in the history of Sino-Nepalese relations to be held in such a high consideration[12].

Thus we see that apart from carrying away the most pleasant memories of their visit to Nepal, the Chinese mission of 1930 failed to make any notable improvement in their mutual relations. In spite of that, the importance of the 1930 Chinese mission lies in the fact that since the Republic, it was the first official mission to Nepal sent by the Chinese government with a view toward renewing friendly relations between these two countries, for the friendly relations between Nepal and China had been interrupted since 1912. Thus the relations between Nepal and China were renewed by this very mission of 1930. Regarding the importance of the Chinese mission of 1932, it can be stated that it was the first special mission to Nepal sent by the Nationalist government of Chiang Kai-Shek for the exclusive purpose of conferring honours upon the Nepalese Prime Minister. Besides that it indeed cemented the existing relations between Nepal and China, resulting in the dispatching of the Chinese missions of 1934 and 1946 to Nepal, and sending the Nepalese mission of 1947 to China. In view of these, the 1930 and 1932 Chinese missions had their own importance in the long history of Sino-Nepalese relations.

***

11 *Ibid.*

12 *Ibid.*

The Chinese Missions of 1934 and 1946 to Nepal*

Following the Nepal-Tibet-China War of 1792, Nepal started sending five-yearly missions to China. This quinquennial mission system continued till 1906. Later on the Nepalese Government decided to terminate over a century old mission system by not dispatching the Nepalese Customary quinquennial mission to China in 1911 on the following grounds: (a) China's claim of Suzerainty over Nepal in 1910, (b) the economically loss in the Nepalese five-yearly trading missions due to China's restrictions upon them, and (c) the Chinese Revolution of 1911 resulting in the overthrow of the Ch'ing dynasty and the establishment of the Republic in China. Even then through tricks China made futile attempts to bring Nepal under their influence. From that period onwards, Nepal became more and more aloof from China and British influence increased in Nepal. In this way from 1914 to 1955, Nepal showed no inclination to maintain relations with China except with the sending of the lone Nepalese goodwill mission to China in April 1947. On the other hand, the Nationalist Government of China made a few feeble attempts to re-establish contacts with the Nepalese Government in the period from 1930 to 1946 by dispatching four missions to Nepal in 1930, 1932, 1934 and 1946 to confer titles and presenting ceremonial robes to the Rana Prime Ministers of Nepal. Regarding those Chinese missions, not much is known about them. Chinese sources which are rarely used by writers

* Published in *Rolamba*, Vol. 16, No. 4 (October-December 1996), pp. 4-8.

and historians shed some new light on this matter. As such, on the basis of those Chinese sources as well as other available Nepalese and Western sources, an attempt is made in this brief paper to discuss the Chinese missions of 1934 and 1946 to Nepal.

The Chinese Mission of 1934 to Nepal

As an expression of the goodwill of the Nationalist Government of China towards Nepal under its new ruler Juddha Shamsher, who assumed the post of Prime Minister of Nepal upon the death of Bhim Shamsher on 1 September, 1932, President Chiang Kai-Shek decided to send a goodwill mission to Nepal to bestow Chinese titles upon the new Nepalese Prime Minister. Juddha Shamsher was also happy to renew relations with the Nationalist Government of China and welcomed their desire to send a mission to Nepal. This time the Chinese mission was headed by Mr. C.P. Liang, the Chinese Consul-General at Calcutta, who was accompanied by Daniel J. Lee, the Vice-Consul. The Chinese mission left Calcutta for Nepal by the end of May 1934 and reached Kathmandu on 2 June, 1934[1].

On 6 June, 1934 an investiture ceremony was held at Tundikhel parade ground in the midst of scenes of great festivity and rejoicing to welcome the Chinese mission. The investiture took place in the presence of the nobility of Nepal, the leading civil and military officers of the Government, professors, doctors, teachers, priests and businessmen[2]. Among the guests present were the British Resident and the members of the British Legation. In spite of the fact that Nepal had suffered an unprecedented earthquake on 15 January 1934, the investiture

---

1 Jenkins Lee, "Chinese Mission To Nepal", *The China Weekly Review*, Shanghai, Vol. 70, 17 November, 1934. p. 400 and *Gorkhapatra*, Nepalese Weekly (now Daily), 1991 B.S. Jestha 26 (8 June, 1934).

2 Ishwari Prasad, *The Life and Times of Maharaja Juddha Shumsher Jung Bahadur Rana of Nepal*, New Delhi: Ashish Publishing House, 1975, p. 121.

ceremony took place in a tent specially arranged for the purpose (instead of the Palace which was damaged by the Great Earthquake) which was as picturesque and important as if it had taken place in a Palace. Prime Minister Juddha Shamsher proceeded from his residence, the Jawalakhel Palace, to the Singha Durbar, the office of the Nepalese Prime Minister, and after dressing himself in the robes of the Grand Master of the Order of *Nepal Tara* reached Tundikhel-- the venue of the investiture ceremony. It was reported that thousands of spectators lined the main streets. It seemed that every one of them wanted to share the joy of his beloved Prime Minister in receiving honours from a country which the Nepalese had always held in high esteem. A salute of twenty one guns was fired when the Chinese mission accompanied by two officers of the Nepalese Government left the Government Guest House. On their arrival at Tundikhel in a State- Carriage escorted by the Nepalese Prime Minister's Mountain body-guards, the royal band played the Chinese national anthem while a guard of honour was presented by the Rifle regiment[3]. A short speech was delivered by the Chinese Envoy C.P. Liang as such:

> "Although this is my first visit to this wonderful country, I do not feel in the least that I am here as a stranger in a strange land. I have come here merely to renew our very old friendship because for centuries the Kingdom of Nepal and China have had friendly intercourse and have been most intimate neighbours. I am unable to express in words how proud I feel to head this important mission to this independent Kingdom with which we are on such cordial terms. The two countries being so closely related geographically, we have much in common as regards our culture, art, literature, religion and many other things in general.

---

3 Lee, f.n. no. 1, p. 400, and Ishwari Prasad, f.n. no. 2, p. 121.

> Therefore, we are neighbours and not strangers. I hope to-day's ceremony will mark another step towards strengthening the ties of goodwill and friendship which already exist between our two countries. On behalf of the President of the National Government of the Republic of China and my fellow countrymen, I respectfully convey to Your Highness the sincerest wish that the prosperity of the Kingdom of Nepal and the welfare of its people will continue under the wise guidance of your Highness. I also wish Your Highness long life and every happiness"[4].

Following the delivery of the speech in Chinese as well as in English, the Chinese Envoy C.P. Liang presented the Nepalese Prime Minister Juddha Shamsher the Order of the First Class *Paoting Hsuan Chiang* and the title of *Luh Chuan Chiang Hsien* (Highest Rank of General in the Chinese Army) on behalf of the President of the National Government of the Chinese Republic[5]. The Nepalese Prime Minister Juddha Shamsher, in turn, expressed his appreciation of the goodwill of the Nationalist Government of China in presenting him such high honours. He also pointed out that the desire to foster mutual goodwill and esteem had always inspired the foreign policy of the Kingdom of Nepal and that it was a pleasure to him to be assured of the friendship of the Republic of China, with which they had had cultural relations for centuries. He made a reference to the first Chinese mission which visited Nepal in 643 A.D.[6]. Before the conclusion of the ceremony, the Commander-in-Chief, Padma Shamsher gave a short speech congratulating the Prime Minister on behalf of the officials of the Nepalese Government and the people of Nepal. When the

---

4 Ishwari Prasad, f.n. no. 2, p. 121.

5 Lee, f.n. no.1, p. 400, See also *Gorkhapatra*, 1991 B.S., Jestha 26 (8 June, 1934).

6 Ishwari Prasad, f.n. no. 2, pp. 121-122.

Chinese mission was leaving Tundikhel, the royal band struck up, while salute of twenty-one guns was fired in honour of the Republic of China[7].

In reciprocating the honours of the National Government of China, another investiture ceremony was performed the next day, i.e., on 7 June, 1934 in presenting to the Chinese Envoy C.P. Liang the insignia of *Nepal Tara* (Bright Star of Nepal) of which he was appointed an Honorary *Pradipta Manyabar*. The Chinese Vice-Consul D.J. Lee was invested with the rank of Honorary *Prabala Gorkha Dakshin Bahu* (Mighty Right Hand of Gorkha)[8]. These honours were presented in the name of the Sovereign after the Chinese party had been introduced to the Nepalese King Tribhuvan Bir Bikram Shah in presence of a large gathering of Princes and nobles[9]. Both the Chinese Envoy and the Chinese Vice-Consul gratefully accepted the proferred honour and said that it was a distinction not bestowed upon them as individuals but as representatives of their country and their nation[10]. The usual ceremonies followed and the function came to an end in the midst of great rejoicing. According to Chinese Vice-Consul D.J. Lee, the Nepalese Prime Minister opined as such:

"The position of Nepal.... secluded, having very little to do with the outside world. Whether Nepal could be benefitted from having a Legation in a foreign country or not remains to be seen. So the establishment of a Nepalese Legation in London is considered an 'experiment'"[11].

During the course of an informal conversation with Chinese Envoy C.P. Liang, Nepalese Prime Minister Juddha Shamsher was reported to have stated that if a Legation was

---

7 Lee, f.n. no. 1, p. 400.

8 *Ibid.*, and Ishwari Prasad, f.n. no. 2, p. 122.

9 Lee, f.n. no. 1, p. 400.

10 Ishwari Prasad, f.n. no. 2, p. 122.

11 Lee, f.n. no. 1, p. 401.

considered to be necessary, Nepal's second Legation abroad would be established in Nanking. The Chinese Vice-Consul D.J. Lee through an article suggested that the Chinese Government should take the initiative step in establishing a Chinese Legation in Nepal and that the Nepalese Government would not hesitate to reciprocate the gesture by establishing a Legation in Nanking without waiting for the result of the 'experiment' of their London Legation[12]. It was also reported that during the last phase of Juddha Shamsher's Premiership in Nepal, Wu Chung-Hsin, the Chinese representative in Tibet, too had tried to resume diplomatic relations between Nepal and China[13]. Meanwhile due to the establishment of a Nepalese Legation in London in May 1934 and the efforts on the part of the Chinese representative in Tibet, Wu Chung-Hsin, there were speculations on possibilities for the resumption of diplomatic relations between Nepal and China. But that did not come about. In spite of that, the Chinese mission of 1934 helped to strengthen the existing relations between Nepal and China, which were revived by the visit of the Chinese missions of 1930 and 1932 to Nepal. The importance of the Chinese mission of 1934 lies in the fact that it was the second Chinese mission sent by the Nationalist Government of China to confer Chinese titles

---

12 *Ibid.*

13 Durga Devi Karki, "Aitihasik Shrota Ra Shrotako Rupma Antarbaarta" (Historical Source and Interview as Source), *Rolamba,* Vol. 9, No. 1 (January-March, 1989), p. 25. She has referred to Chung Lin Hsin as the Chinese Commissioner in Tibet. But this is not correct. The Western sources prove that it was Wu Chung-Hsin, Chairman of the Mongolian and Tibetan Affairs Commission, who was sent by the Chinese Government as its representative in Tibet to attend the installation ceremonies of the Fourteenth Dalai Lama. It seems that the Chinese representative (envoy) Wu Chung-Hsin arrived at Lhasa in the middle of January 1940. After attending the installation ceremonies of the Fourteenth Dalai Lama in February 1940, by 15 April, 1940, Wu had left Lhasa, leaving as Chinese representative Dr. Kung Ch'ing-Tsung. For the details of the Wu Chung-Hsin mission, see Alastair Lamb, *Tibet, China & India 1914-1950,* Hertfordshire: Roxford Books, 1989, pp. 282-289. See also, H.E. Richardson, *Tibet and Its History,* London: Oxford University Press, 1962, pp. 151-157.

on the newly inaugurated Rana Prime Minister Juddha Shamsher and to renew Nepal-China ties. Besides that both members of the Chinese mission, the Chinese Envoy C.P. Liang and the Chinese Vice-Consul D.J. Lee were given with Nepalese titles.

As regards the Chinese mission of 1934, here it is appropriate to examine the viewpoint of a writer who opined that following the death of the Thirteenth Dalai Lama in December 1933 and the selection of the Regent, a Chinese mission headed by General Huang Mu-Sung came to Lhasa and after congratulating the Regent, the Chinese mission came to Nepal from Lhasa and bestowed the Chinese titles upon Nepalese Prime Minister Juddha Shamsher. To quote him:

> "In 1990 B.S. (1933 A.D.) Tibet's Supreme Ruler the Thirteenth Dalai Lama passed away. A new Regent was selected to rule the country and installed. On that occasion, a Chinese mission headed by General Huang Mu-Sung came to Lhasa from Peking. After completing its work in Lhasa of congratulating the new Regent, the Chinese mission also came to Nepal from Lhasa. In Nepal, the Chinese mission conferred the highest military ranks in the Chinese Army and title "Itang Pao-t'ing Hsuan Chian" and "Lun Chiang Shang Chiang" upon *Sri Tin Maharaja* Juddha Shamsher in *Kartik-Mangsir* 1991 B.S. (October-November 1934)"[14]

The above statement seems faulty on the following grounds. First of all, it is a well-established fact that it was not the Chinese mission headed by General Huang Mu-Sung to confer Chinese titles upon Nepalese Prime Minister Juddha

14 Jnanmani Nepal, *Nepal-Bhot-Chin Sambandha Ka Kehi Sanskritik Paksha* (Some Cultural Aspects of Nepal-Tibet China Relations), Kathmandu: Royal Nepal Academy, 2045 B.S., p. 398.

Shamsher. Mr. C.P. Liang, the Chinese Consul-General at Calcutta, who had led the Chinese mission of 1934, had actually conferred these Chinese titles upon Nepalese Prime Minister Juddha Shamsher[15]. After the death of the Thirteenth Dalai Lama in December 1933, the Nationalist Government of China expressed grief at the loss of the Dalai Lama and conferred a posthumous title on him. Besides that, a special mission of condolence, headed by a Senior Chinese General, Huang Mu-Sung, who had been President Chiang Kai-Shek's Vice Chief of the General Staff, was sent to Lhasa in January 1934. General Huang arrived at Lhasa on 28 August, 1934 and left the Tibetan capital on 28 November 1934. While returning to China *via* India, he seemed to have just visited Nepal on the way[16]. Secondly, generally it was not feasible for Chinese General Huang Mu-sung, leading a special mission of condolence, to confer Chinese titles on the newly appointed Nepalese Prime Minister Juddha Shamsher. Thirdly, the investiture upon the Nepalese Prime Minister took place in Kathmandu not in *Kartik-Mangsir* 1991 B.S. (October-November, 1934) but on 24 Jestha, 1991 B.S. (6 June, 1934)[17]. Therefore, on the basis of Chinese, Nepalese and Western sources, it can be concluded that the Chinese mission headed by Mr. C.P. Liang, the Chinese Consul-General at Calcutta, had bestowed Chinese titles upon Nepalese Prime Minister Juddha Shamsher on 6 June, 1934.

---

15 Lee, f.n. no. 1, pp. 400-401.

16 General Huang seemed to have reached China by February 1935 and in March 1935 he was appointed Chairman of the Mongolian and Tibetan Affairs Commission. For the details of the Huang Mu-Sung mission, See Lamb, f.n. no. 13, pp. 231-269. See also Michael C.Van Walt Van Praag, *The Status of Tibet,* Colorado: Westview Press, 1987, pp. 68-70, and Richardson, f.n. no. 13, pp. 141-143.

17 *Gorkhapatra*, 1991 B.S. Jestha 26, (8 June, 1934), Lee, f.n. no. 1, p. 400, and Ishwari Prasad. f.n. no. 2, p. 120

The Chinese Mission of 1946 to Nepal

After 1934, the Chinese Nationalist Government sent a goodwill mission to Nepal only in 1946, after a gap of twelve years, for political turmoil in China and the beginning of the Second World War had precluded further contact between the two countries, and it was not until the end of the Second World War in December 1945 that any overture was made. Meanwhile here it should be mentioned that during the Second World War, President Chiang Kai-Shek visited India in February 1942, mainly to try to rally British support for the Kuomintang against Japan. During that visit, he also met the Nepalese Envoy to India, Bahadur Shamsher, and talked about the possibility of renewing relations between Nepal and China on the basis of equality[18]. Besides that, during President Chiang Kai-Shek's visit to India, Nepalese Prime Minister Juddha Shamsher gave fifty thousand rupees ($10,000) to the Chinese Red Cross Fund as a friendly gesture of Nepalese Government's towards the Nationalist Government of China[19].

The Nationalist Government of China sent a goodwill mission to Nepal in 1946 under the leadership of Shen Tsung-lien, Private Secretary to President Chiang Kai-Shek[20].

---

18 Niranjan Bhattarai, *Chin Ra Tyasasita Nepal Ko Sambandha* (China and Her Relations with Nepal), Kathmandu: Nepal Academy, 2018 B.S., p. 231.

19 Asad Husain, *British India's Relations with the Kingdom of Nepal,* London: George Allen and Unwin Ltd., 1970, p. 222.

20 T.R. Ghoble, *China-Nepal Relations and India,* New Delhi: Deep and Deep Publications, 1986, p. 32, and Kaisher Bahadur K.C., *Nepal After the Revolution of 1950*, Vol. I, Kathmandu: Sharada Prakashan Griha, 1976, p. 54. It seems that before leading the Chinese mission of 1946 to Nepal, Shen Tsung-lien, who was close to President Chiang Kai-Shek, had headed the Chinese Cultural and Educational Mission to India in 1943. In January 1944, he was appointed Chairman of the Mongolian and Tibetan Affairs Commission. He had also served as the Chinese Government's representative in Lhasa from August 1944 to January 1946. Here it should be pointed out that Shen Tsung-lien was a scholar who had studied at both Harvard and the Sorbonne before

The Chinese mission arrived in Kathmandu on 26 November, 1946 and presented the insignia of *Teh Tsung Dah Sew Pao Ting Hsun Chang* (Grand Order of the Second Tripod) to the newly appointed Nepalese Prime Minister Padma Shamsher and the Grand Order of the Cloud and the Banner to Commander-in-Chief Mohan Shamsher[21]. The Chinese mission brought various presents and the message of the Nationalist Government of China to the Nepalese Prime Minister Padma Shamsher[22].

The importance of the Chinese mission of 1946 lies in the fact that it was the last Chinese mission sent by the Nationalist Government of China to Nepal to renew Sino-Nepalese relations after a gap of twelve years, and also the last Chinese mission to confer Chinese titles upon the Rana Prime Minister of Nepal. Besides that, it was due to this Chinese mission of 1946 also, that the Nepalese Government also dispatched a mission to China in 1947 for the first time in forty one years.

***

---

holding senior academic appointments at Chinese Universities. Later on he, with his assistant Liu Shen-Chi wrote a book about Tibet, *Tibet and the Tibetans*, Stanford, California: Stanford University Press, 1953. For the details about Shen Tsung-lien, see Lamb, f.n. no. 13, pp. 328-349.

21 Rishikesh Shah, *Modern Nepal: A Political History 1885-1955*, Vol. II, New Delhi: Manohar Publications, 1990, p. 170.

22 Nepal, f.n. no. 14, p. 398.

Republic China's Intrigues Against Nepal*

It is interesting to note that in the past Imperial China did not claim the right of suzerainty over Nepal. Only after the Nepal-China Peace Agreement of 1792 (which ended the Sino-Nepalese war of 1792), did the idea of suzerainty seem to have entered the minds of the then rulers of Imperial China, after which they nurtured the concept for a long time. In 1910, for the first time, Imperial China formally asserted its claim of suzerainty over Nepal openly. That Chinese claim was proved baseless when it was challenged by both the Nepalese and the British India Governments. In spite of that, Republic China could not resist the temptation to reiterate and reinforce the right of suzerainty over Nepal again and again. In 1913, the New Republic of China invited Nepal to join China in a union of the "Five Affiliated Races" (the Chinese, Manchus, Mongolians, Tibetans and Muslims). By turning down the offer of the Republic Chinese government, Nepalese Prime Minister Chandra Shamsher foiled China's intrigue against Nepal in connection with China's attempt to claim and establish its suzerainty over Nepal. That episode of 1913 clearly indicates that, notwithstanding the changed political scenario in China, the Chinese tried, through their attempted intrigues, to bring Nepal under their influence; and that it did not affect the official viewpoint of Republic China with respect to Nepal. Till now, the episode of 1913, relating to Republic China's intrigues against Nepal has not yet been properly discussed by anyone. In view of this, an attempt is made in this paper to discuss

* Published in *Voice of History*, Vol. XIII, No. 1 (July 1998), pp. 57-68.

Republic China's intrigues against Nepal in 1913 -- an important episode of Nepal-China relations.

Significantly enough, as late as 1908 -- four years after Colonel Younghusband had led a successful expedition to Lhasa in 1904 and compelled the Tibetan authorities to agree -- China's special Commissioner to Tibet, Chang Yin-t'ang sought to assert the Chinese claim of suzerainty over Nepal. Following the establishment of Chinese authority in Tibet in 1910, the British government, for request by the Nepalese government, raised the question of protecting Nepalese interests in Tibet, which were greatly threatened by Chinese interference in the internal administration of Tibet. At that time, the Chinese for the first time formally claimed that Nepal "has been a tributary to China and has long submitted vassalage to China"[1], and for this reason, she declined to settle the matter with the British government. The Nepalese government repudiated the Chinese claims vehemently. Upon the British government's request, the Nepalese government furnished the history of Sino-Nepalese relations from ancient times, but the British found the Chinese claims to be not quite strong enough. On the other hand, the British government found the Nepalese government's total refutation and vehement contradictions of all Chinese claims in that regard to be sufficiently strong. The British government had guaranteed to protect Nepal's interests in Tibet, which were under direct threat from Chinese subversion. Moreover, Nepal was her ally, and any encroachment upon her freedom, sovereignty and integrity by China would have had adverse repercussions in the area. As such, the British government conveyed to China its rejection of the Chinese claims, as well as its determination to check any attempt on the part of China to enforce 'her suzerainty' over Nepal[2]. The Chinese government

1 Note from Wai-wu-pu, 28 October 1910, Foreign Sec. E., January 1911, No. 197, National Archives of India (NAI), New Delhi.

2 J.N. Jordan to Prince Ching, 10 May 1911, Foreign Sec. E, July 1911, No. 279, NAI.

also tried to exert its best efforts on the diplomatic front in order to support its claim. The diplomatic tussle lasted for some time. With the outbreak of the 1911 Revolution in China and the expulsion of the Chinese from Tibet, the question of Nepal's status *vis-a-vis* China became purely academic. The Chinese Revolution also provided an excuse for the Nepalese government to terminate over a century old quinquennial mission system to China.

Here it should be mentioned that with the fall of the Ch'ing Empire (Dynasty) and the establishment of the Chinese Republic on 1 January, 1912, the situation completely changed in Tibet as well. For in 1911, when the Tibetans fought the Ch'ing troops in Tibet, it was Nepalese mediation that eventually led to the Sino-Tibetan agreements of August and December 1912 paving the way for the safe withdrawal of General Chung Yin as well as the safe return of the Chinese garrison from Tibet. But the significant point to be noted was that even at that time, China had not given up her claim of suzerainty over Nepal, for the Chinese tried to bring Nepal under their control through their attempted intrigues. Yuan Shih-Kai, the newly-elected President of the New Republic of China and General Chung Yin, the Senior officer on duty in Tibet, exchanged communications, clearly suggesting that the new Chinese regime had not yet changed its viewpoint about Nepal being a tributary state of China. Interestingly, in a secret telegram dated 1 February, 1913 to Thinyik Company for transmission to the President of the Chinese Republic, which was reported to have been intercepted by British intelligence in Calcutta, General Chung Yin had mentioned Nepal as "practically the last of our tributary states"[3] which the new Chinese Republic regime could not afford to lose to the British. The Chinese General also pointed out that if the Nepalese could

3 Kanchanmoy Mojumdar, *Political Relations between India and Nepal 1877-1923*, New Delhi: Munshiram Manoharlal Publishers Pvt. Ltd. 1973, p. 182 and Michael C. Van Walt Van Praag, *The Status of Tibet* Colorado: Westview Press, 1987, p. 76 and p. 237.

be persuaded to send a delegation for "orders and advice" to Peking, then "there would be proof positive that Nepal is subject to the Republic". He also argued that from the military point of view, the Nepalese alliance would also strengthen the Chinese Republic. Meanwhile, General Chung also suspected that the Nepalese Prime Minister Chandra Shamsher had already made an offensive and defensive alliance with the British, but he was not completely sure if it had made him a "mere puppet of the British"[4]. It seems that on 1 February, 1913, General Chung Yin also sent another telegram (this one was not intercepted) to Yuan Shih-Kai, the President of the Chinese Republic. In that telegram to Peking, the Chinese General recommended the despatch to Nepal of a special mission "to explain matters". A union of Nepal with the "Five Affiliated Races of China", General Chung argued, was of great importance, as" the relations between China and Nepal during the past several hundred years have been unceasingly more intimate than between China and Tibet"[5]. Going through the intercepted telegram from Peking to Thinyik Company for transmission to General Chung, it becomes evident that the Chinese government had indeed encouraged General Chung's efforts[6]. While welcoming General Chung's proposal, President Yuan Shih-Kai remarked that rightly, if Nepal "could be drawn into alliance with China", it would be the "most fitting consequence of her loyalty" to the new Republic[7] and that the Nepalese Prime Minister Chandra Shamsher as an ally of China might be an effective balance against the pro-British Dalai Lama. Being aware of the risks of Chung's proposal, the Chinese President also pointed out that it was quite certain that the British would strongly oppose that new Chinese plot and therefore he cautioned General Chung that British annoyance would make the more important Tibetan issue harder to settle. For that

---

4 Mojumdar, f.n. no.3., p. 182.
5 See Appendix A
6 Van Walt Van Praag, f.n. no. 3, p. 237.
7 Mojumdar, f.n. no. 3, p. 182.

reason, President Yuan asked General Chung to be very cautious while trying to win over the Nepalese Premier[8].

It was against this background that from Yatung, near the Tibet-Sikkim border, General Chung Yin wrote a letter dated 23 February, 1913 (*Vide* the cover of the letter) to Nepalese Prime Minister Chandra Shamsher, a Chinese communication very similar to the one sent to the Dalai Lama[9], proposing the "Union of Nepal with the Five Affiliated Races of China" as well as suggesting the despatch by Nepal of " a special delegation with congratulations to Peking for orders and advice"[10]. Here it should be mentioned that this letter, along with the unintercepted telegram originally in Chinese and its English translations, were sent from Yatung by General Chung in a cover addressed to Prime Minister Chandra Shamsher and were handed over to Nepalese *Subedar* Run Gumbhir Singh who, had accompanied the Chinese General from Lhasa[11]. Both the aforementioned letters were received by Premier Chandra Shamsher around 6 March, 1913. Undoubtedly the Chinese General had expressed his desire for the continuance of the old relationship as existing heretofore between China and Nepal. Meanwhile the Nepalese Premier was fully aware of the meaning and significance of the Chinese General's letters, that is, General Chung was evidently attempting to revive the Chinese notion of Nepal to be her feudatory. The Nepalese government had been repudiating the Chinese claim of suzerainty over Nepal since 1910. The Nepalese Prime Minister had no wish to change his government's recent attitude towards China and annoy the British government, for Premier Chandra Shamsher did not want Nepal to become a feudal state of China

---

8 *Ibid.*, pp. 182-183.

9 On 21 April, 1912, the Chinese President Yuan Shih-Kai had issued an order inducing Tibet to form a union of the "Five Races" (the Chinese, Manchus, Mongolians, Tibetans and Turkiks (or Muslims). For the text of the Presidential order, See Van Walt Van Praag, f.n. no. 3, p. 51.

10 See Appendix C

11 See Appendix B

at all. That is why he characterised the Chinese proposal as simply ' absurd'[12]. On 10 March, 1913, the Nepalese Prime Minister Chandra Shamsher met H.L. Showers, the officiating British Resident in Nepal. On that occasion not only did he hand over the aforementioned original and translated Chinese letters from General Chung and a memorandum prepared by him concerning his proposed reply to the Chinese General, but also discussed his proposed reply to the Chinese General with the officiating British Resident[13]. In the course of his talks with Chandra Shamsher, H.L. Showers pointed out that considering that General Chung had apparently written entirely on his own authority and that he had practically ceased to be *Amban* or Resident from the time of his withdrawal from Lhasa in December 1912, the proposals made by General Chung hardly deserved to be treated quite as seriously as they had been. Here it should be mentioned that on 11 March, 1913, H.L. Showers reported to the Secretary to the Government of India all the details regarding his meeting with Premier Chandra Shamsher on 10 March, 1913 and also forwarded all the original Chinese and translated English letters from General Chung and Chandra Shamsher's memorandum regarding his proposed reply to General Chung. He also informed him that the Nepalese Prime Minister had rejected the main Chinese proposal in clear terms and that the Nepalese government's communication to General Chung would be despatched on 16 March, 1913[14]. While reporting, the officiating British Resident remarked that a noteworthy point was that a period of twenty two days had apparently elapsed between the date of General Chung's telegram to Peking and that of the Chinese General's letter to the Nepalese Prime Minister, the inference being that the Chinese government had possibly authorised General Chung's despatch

---

12 *Ibid.*

13 H.L. Showers to Secretary, Government of India, 11 March 1913, Foreign Dept. Sec. External, August 1913, No. 240, NAI.

14 *Ibid.*

of the communication to Nepal[15]. From that it can be assumed that he was not aware of the British government's interception of his telegram from Peking to Thinyik Company for transmission to General Chung. Here it should be noted that the British officiating Resident also believed that the Nepalese government's reply would prove useful serving to demonstrate the futility of any inclination there might have been on the part of China to disregard the terms of the message conveyed to them by the British government on 10 May, 1911 as to their claim to suzerainty over Nepal[16]. Interestingly, the British Indian government transmitted a copy of the correspondence regarding Chinese intrigues against Nepal to its Home Government at London, to the Army Department and British Political officer in Sikkim[17], as well as to the British Minister at Peking[18]. Significantly enough J.N. Jordan, the British Minister at Peking, requested for Secretary to the Government of India to supply him with a copy of the text of the reply returned by the Nepalese Premier to General Chung, if that should be available[19].

Another noteworthy point was that although Chandra Shamsher rejected the main Chinese proposal in clear terms he was desirous of making his reply as courteous and conciliatory as possible, because he was anxious about the position of the Nepalese community in Lhasa and with the future of Tibet still uncertain, he did not wish his relations with the Chinese representatives to be other than amicable. Therefore, a small amendment in the reply suggested by the officiating British

---

15 *Ibid.*

16 *Ibid.*

17 Memorandum by the office of Secretary, Government of India, Foreign Department Sec. External, August 1913, No. 242, NAI.

18 Deputy Secretary, Govt. of India to His Britannic Majesty's Minister at Peking, 11 April 1913, Foreign Department Sec. External, August 1913, No. 244, NAI.

19 J.N. Jordan to Secretary, Govt. of India 23 May, 1913, Foreign Dept. Sec. External, August 1913, No. 246, NAI.

Resident was accepted by the Nepalese Prime Minister[20]. Thus, although he turned down General Chung's proposal, on 16 March 1913 Prime Minister Chandra Shamsher sent a most courteous and at the same delicately sarcastic reply stating that "as Nepal is an ancient Hindu Kingdom, desirous of preserving her independence and her separate existence, she cannot entertain the idea of such a union with the Five Affiliated Races said to constitute the Republic of China"[21]. In this way, General Chung Yin failed in his efforts to draw Nepal into an alliance with China and returned to China empty-handed[22]. Meanwhile, as concerns the request of the British Indian government[23], the officiating British Resident obtained from the Nepalese Prime Minister a copy of the text of the reply returned by him to General Chung. While supplying the said document, the Nepalese Premier asked the officiating British Resident to treat that document as strictly confidential. The officiating British Resident forwarded a copy of the text of the Nepalese Premier's reply dated 16 March, 1913 to the proposals made by General Chung to the Secretary to the Government of India[24], who also transmitted a copy of the said text to its Home Government[25] as well as to the British Mission in Peking[26].

---

20 H.L. Showers to Secretary, Govt. of India, 11 March 1913, Foreign Dept. Sec. External, August 1913, No. 240, NAI.

21 See Appendix D

22 Here it should be noted that General Chung, having lost hold of Central Tibet, foolishly returned to China and President Yuan Shih-Kai had him put to death in 1915. Alastair Lamb, *Tibet, China & India 1914-1950*, Hertfordshire: Rexford Books, 1989, p. 78.

23 Deputy Secretary, Govt. of India to the Resident in Nepal, 30 June 1913, Foreign Dept. Sec. External, August 1913, No. 247, NAI.

24 H.L. Showers to Secretary, Govt. of India, 11 July 1913, Foreign Dept. Sec. External, August 1913, No. 248, NAI.

25 Memorandum by the office of Secretary, Govt. of India, Foreign Dept. Sec. External, August 1913, No. 250, NAI.

26 Secretary, Govt. of India to His Britannic Majesty's Charge d'Affairs, Peking, 17 July 1913, Foreign Dept. Sec. External, August 1913, No. 249, NAI.

In this way, we see that by rejecting the Chinese idea altogether, the Nepalese Prime Minister foiled Chinese intrigues in Nepal in connection with Chinese attempt to claim and establish authority over Nepal. With this, the diplomatic manoeuvre between England and China since 1910 over the chapter of the Chinese claim of suzerainty over Nepal was also ruled out for all practical purposes in 1913. Even by 1911 Nepal had stopped the over-a-century old system of sending quinquennial missions to China. Meanwhile, the Nepalese reply was indeed a matter of great satisfaction to the British government, for it was sent only after consultation with the officiating British Resident. Due to their policy in Nepal in connection with their paramount interest in the Himalayan area, the Chinese intrigues against Nepal in 1913 had been of great concern to the British government. Therefore, being content with the action taken by Nepalese, the British government conveyed to the Nepalese Prime Minister an expression of satisfaction with the nature of the reply and their appreciation of the frank manner in which he had placed the correspondence before them[27]. Besides that, the British government also informed the Nepalese Premier of the new British policy towards Tibet stating that in view of the earnest desire of the British government to re-establish peace and harmony between China and Tibet and to preserve the ancient rights and privileges of the Tibetans, they had invited the Chinese and Tibetan governments to a joint conference to be held at Darjeeling, at an early date, for the settlement of the Tibetan question by means of an agreement to which all three governments would be signatories[28]. After the episode of 1913 relating to China's

---

27 H.L. Showers to Secretary, Govt. of India, 11 March 1913, Foreign Dept. Sec. External, August 1913, No. 240, NAI, and Deputy Secretary, Govt. of India to H.L. Showers, 25 March, Foreign Dept. Sec. External, August 1913, No. 241, NAI.

28 Deputy Secretary, Govt. of India to H.L. Showers, 11 June 1913, Foreign Dept. Sec. External, August 1913, No. 245, NAI.

intrigues against Nepal, Nepal became more and more afar from China and British influence increased in Nepal.

Lastly here it would not be out of context to mention that even after the events of 1913, the Chinese made some further attempts to revive their claim over Nepal. For instance, in 1916, Dr. Sun Yat Sen, the founder of the Chinese Republic, citing a long list of so-called lost territories, including Nepal, noted that he would reclaim them[29]. Similarly in 1924, in reply to an inquiry by Perceval Landon about the Chinese attitude towards the quinquennial missions from Nepal, Dr. Wellington Koo (Ku Wei-chun), the Chinese Foreign Minister, wrote that though formerly the "tribute" came from Nepal once in five years, it was later on agreed that it should come once in twelve years[30]. Though the new agreement referred to by the Chinese Foreign Minister was a fictitious one, it showed that China had no intention of giving up her claim to Nepal. The last Chinese attempt to revive the Chinese claim over Nepal was made by Mao-Tse-Tung in 1939[31]. It seems that the Chinese attempts to claim Nepal inevitably raised apprehension in Nepal. As a result from 1914 to 1955, Nepal showed no inclination to maintain relations with China except with the sending of a lone Nepalese goodwill mission to China in April 1947. During that period relations with China were limited to the reception of Chinese missions to Kathmandu in 1930, 1932, 1934 and 1946 sent to confer titles and to present ceremonial robes to the Prime Ministers of Nepal. Thus, from the foregoing discussion it can be concluded that the events of 1913 relating to Chinese intrigues against Nepal were an important episode in the annals of Nepal-China relations, for it brought about a turning point in

---

29 Poorna Bahadur M.A., *Nepal Behind the Screen,* Kathmandu: Nepal Youth League, Central Committee, 1957, pp. 15-16.

30 Perceval Landon, *Nepal*, Vol. 2, Kathmandu: Ratna Pustak Bhandar, Reprint, 1987, pp. 102-103.

31 Girilal Jain, *India Meets China in Nepal,* Bombay: Asia Publishing House, 1959, pp. 106-107.

Sino-Nepalese relations leading to the severing of official relations between the two countries till 1955.

Appendix A*

(Translation)

Telegram, dated the 1st February 1913

From ----- His Excellency General Chung, Chinese Resident of Tibet

To ----- His Excellency the President of China

The relations between China and Nepal during the past several hundred years have been unceasingly more intimate than between China and Tibet.

It is praiseworthy that during the seige of Lhasa His Highness the Maharaja of Nepal twice sent officers to intercede and sent officers and men to escort the Chinese leaving Lhasa.

As the Chinese Republic has been founded it is desirable that a special delegation should be sent to Nepal to explain matters.

---

* Source : Foreign Department Sec. External, August 1913, No. 240, National Archives of India (NAI), New Delhi.

The present Maharaja is a very well-informed ruler and is making strenuous efforts to build up power and prosperity. The standard of his subjects is a million times higher than the Tibetans. Unfortunately the territory under His Highness's rule is small and there is no navy, but if a union could be effected with the Five Affiliated Races of China the future prospects will be very bright.

Awaiting telegraphic reply.

Appendix B*

Memorandum

This is a translation of a letter in Chinese received from General Chung from Yatung. Both the letter in Chinese and its English rendering were sent by the said General in a cover addressed to me and handed over to our Subadar Run Gumbhir Sing who has accompanied him from Lhasa. The letter will speak for itself.

After mentioning the recent Change in the form of Government in China and expressing appreciation of our help in connection with the cessation of hostilities in Tibet, the latter gives expression to a desire for the continuance of the old relationship as existing hithertofore between China and Nepal

* Source: Foreign Department Sec. External, August 1913, No. 240, NAI.

and then proceeds to hint at a union with the five races, and idea, which to say the least of it is simply absurd. It is intended to send a reply to it to the effect that we are glad that the help rendered by us in connection with the recent hostilities in Tibet has been appreciated that as Nepal wishes to always remain in peace and amity with her friends and neighbours so long as her independence is respected, and as her friendly relations with China are of such a long date it is only natural that she should be glad at the continuance of the same; and that as Nepal is an ancient Hindu Kingdom, desirous of preserving her independence and her separate existence she cannot entertain the idea of a union with the Five Affiliated Races said to constitute the Republic of China.

Appendix C*

(Translation of Despatch)

Dated Yatung, the February 1913

From ---- His Excellency General Chung, Chinese Resident of Tibet

To ---- His Highness the Maharaja of Nepal

Source : Foreign Department Sec. External, August 1913, No. 240, NAI.

May it please Your Highness,

I have the honour to inform Your Highness that the Government of China has undergone a complete change from absolute monarchy to a republic of the Five Affiliated Races; His Excellency the President of the Chinese Republic has been elected by the people as the Chief Executive of the Nation and the New National Flag of five coloured stripes, to wit, red, yellow, blue, white and black, has been unfurled to the loud acclamations and bewilderment, of many Foreign Powers who contemplate early recognition.

Inasmuch as the relations between Nepal and China have always been most intimate and cordial, as clearly shown by the services rendered in connection with the cessation of hostilities at Lhasa, the facts of which have been duly communicated by telegraph to the President who most highly appreciate such kindly acts, and, furthermore, as Nepal is a country small in extent, but noted for good fighting forces, it is desirable that at least the same relationship should exist as hithertofore, and, if a union of Nepal with the Five Affiliated Races of China could be effected, China may be regarded as Nepalese China, the needs of one part will be felt and responded to by the rest of the nation, and the powers of China, thus united, may be so multiplied that it will be difficult to draw a parallel.

It is with great satisfaction that I have the opportunity to record my observations concerning Your Highness's profound Knowledge of the affairs of the World and untiring efforts for building up a powerful and prosperous nation.

On this, the rare and unique occasion when China has adopted this Republic form of Government after the example of the great Republic of the United States of America on a firm basis, it is expected that it may please Your Highness to despatch a special delegation with congratulations to Peking for orders and advice or to forward to me for transmission to Peking any memorial Your Highness may be pleased to despatch.

[ ] Seal of the Resident.

Appendix D

Dated the 16th March 1913

From ---- His Highness Maharaja Major General Sir Chandra Shumshere Jung Bahadur Rana, G.C. B., G.C.S.I., G.C.V.O., D.C.L., Honorary Colonel of the 4th Gurkhas, Thong-lin-pimma-ko-Kang-Wang-Syan, Prime Minister and Marshal of Nepal.

To ---- His Excellency General Chung, Camp Yatung.

After Compliments :-

* Source : Foreign Department Sec. External, August 1913, No. 248, NAI

I have received Your Excellency's kind letter sent from Camp Yatung, and understood the contents thereof. It is with very great pleasure that we have heard that the help rendered by us in connection with the recent hostilities in Tibet has been appreciated. Nepal has no other wish but to ever remain in peace and amity with her friends and neighbours so long as her independence is respected and as her friendly relations with China are of such a long date it is only natural that she should be glad at the continuance of the same.

With regard to the question of union with the Five Races of China I am sorry that as Nepal is an ancient Hindu Kingdom, desirous of preserving her independence and her separate existence she cannot entertain the idea of such a union with the Five Affiliated Races said to constitute the Republic of China. What more shall I write to Your Excellency who is yourself a fountain-head of wisdom. We wish Your Excellency's welfare.

***

The Political Status of Nepal *Vis-a-vis* China*

This article is devoted specifically to raising a few related questions on the much debated question of the political status of Nepal *vis-a-vis* China. To what extent did the Sino-Nepalese Agreement of 1792 (Treaty of Betravati) and the Nepalese-Tibetan treaty of 1856 (Treaty of Thapathali) really support the Chinese claim of suzerainty over Nepal ? Did Nepal's quinquennial missions to China with "tributes" entail Nepal's political subordination to China ? And finally, did the reception of Chinese robes, titles and honours by Nepalese rulers as well as the submissive language and expressions of the Nepalese letters addressed to Chinese court establish Chinese lordship over Nepal? These are evidently very controversial questions. This article is an attempt to deal with political status of Nepal *vis-a-vis* China on the basis of available Nepalese, Tibetan, Western and translated Chinese sources.

In order to teach Nepal a lesson for her aggressive behaviour towards Tibet, the Manchu Emperor, Ch'ien Lung sent a large army under the command of General Fu K'ang-an. The Chinese army attacked Nepal unrelentingly and defeated the Nepalese army. Finally a peace agreement was concluded between Nepal and China in September 1792.

---

* Published in *Voice of History*, Vol. IX-XI, No. 1 (December 1986), pp. 8-18.

The Nepalese and the Chinese gave different interpretations of the peace agreement of 1792 (Treaty of Betravati). Chinese authorities and scholars claim that Nepal had accepted Chinese suzerainty in the peace agreement of 1792[1], which is strongly denied by the Nepalese side. Some of the terms of the 1792 agreement would readily indicate the recognition by Nepal of some superior status on the part of China, but it is doubtful that this recognition had any legal validity, for one of the most important provisions of the agreement, Article 4, was not adhered to by China, as she did not come to the help of Nepal upon the latter's request at the time of the Anglo-Nepalese war of 1814-1816. The Chinese *Amban*(Resident) at Lhasa on behalf of the Peking Court wrote "When you (Nepal) fight with the British this happens outside our borders. The soldiers of the Emperor cannot go there"[2]. The Nepalese had the same experience with the Chinese *Amban's* rejection of the Nepalese request for military assistance against the British in India in 1842[3]. This attitude on the part of China goes against the very concept of suzerainty. Here it can be argued that refusal by China to comply with the most important provision of the agreement barred her from claiming any rights that might have been hers under it. Thus the Chinese

1 Schyler Cammann, *Trade Through The Himalayas*, Princeton, New Jersey: Princeton University Press, 1951, p. 131, Chusei Suzuki, "China's Relations with Inner Asia: The Hsiung-Nu, Tibet", in John K. Fairbank (ed.), *The China World Order*, Cambridge, Massachusetts: Harvard University Press, 1970, p. 193, C.Y.W. Meng, "China's Interest in the Complications between Tibet and Nepal", *The China Weekly Review*, 26 April 1930, p. 329, and Denis Twitchett and John K. Fairbank (General editors), *The Cambridge History of China*, Vol. 10, Late Ch'ing 1800-1911, Part I, Cambridge: Cambridge University Press, 1978, p. 103.

2 Yogi Narahari Nath, *Itihas Prakash* (Lights on History), Part I, Kathmandu: Nepal Press, 2012 B.S., pp. 91-92.

3 Leo E.Rose, "Sino-Indian Rivalry and the Himalayan Border States", *Orbis*, Vol. V, No. 2, July 1961, The Quarterly Journal of World Affairs, University of Pennsylvania, p. 202.

government, while claiming suzerainty over Nepal, had clearly given up any responsibility which a suzerain owed to a vassal.

According to Article I, Nepal had agreed to treat the Chinese Emperor as arbitrator for any dispute between her and Tibet. Assigning this position to China, however, does not imply acceptance of China's suzerainty. It should be noted that in International Law, acceptance of arbitration by a third power does not mean acceptance of the suzerainty of that third power in any way. Moreover, the arbitration clause under discussion in the agreement of 1792 between Nepal and Tibet was never treated as binding in subsequent practice, and it remained a dead letter. Neither Nepal nor Tibet gave any practical importance to it, as is clear from the fact that disputes did arise between the two neighbours from time to time, but neither ever cared to put them before the Chinese throne for arbitration. Even when tension between them reached its highest point in 1854 and the dispute could not be solved amicably, instead of referring their dispute to China, Nepal and Tibet again went to war in 1855-1856. Rather it would be interesting to note that Nepal acted as a mediator at the time of the Sino-Tibetan Crisis of 1911-1912[4], paving the way for the safe withdrawal of Chinese troops from Tibet. It would not have been possible for Nepal to mediate in that crisis had she been a tributary of China.

To sum up the above discussion, the aforementioned agreement of 1792 proved of little utility in determining the relations between Nepal and China. The agreement cannot be interpreted in any way that would give China's suzerain rights over Nepal. Moreover, the agreement became abrogated by the subsequent conduct of the parties, specially in the year 1855, when the war between Nepal and Tibet put an end to it. This

---

4 Alastair Lamb, *The Mac Mohan Line*, Vol. II, London: Routledge and Kegan Paul, 1966, pp. 371-385 and Prem R. Uprety, *Nepal-Tibet Relations 1850-1930*, Kathmandu: Puga Nara, 1980, pp. 127-139.

war of 1855 culminated in the Nepalese-Tibetan Treaty of 1856. China remained neutral this time, and the Nepalese fully avenged their early defeat of 1792 by compelling the Tibetans to pay Rs. 10,000 annually as tribute to Nepal and by securing extraterritorial rights for the Nepalese traders. The very result of China's non-interference in the war waged by Nepal against Tibet establishes two things (a) Nepal was successful in her attempt to make China neutral in her (Nepal's) action against Tibet (b) Nepal was a sovereign power independent of China in exercising her sovereign rights.

After the conclusion of the Treaty of Thapathali of 1856, the Chinese *Amban* acted as the mediator, and there is a reference to the Emperor of China in the preamble of this treaty. There is great controversy about the translation and the exact meaning of the language used in the preamble. Several translations of the treaty from both the Tibetan and Nepalese texts have used the expression that "the Emperor shall continue to be regarded with respect", whereas others have translated the preamble as "the Emperor of China shall be obeyed by both states as before"[5]. The Treaty of Thapathali of 1856 is one of the most important documentary basis of the Chinese claim of suzerainty over Nepal. The Chinese version is that Nepal and Tibet, having "obeyed" the Emperor of China "as before" and "borne allegiance" to him "up to the present time", as translated by Ramsay, laid stress on the subordination of Nepal and Tibet to China[6]. But O'Connor's version (translation) indicated that both Tibet and Nepal had paid only "respect" to the Emperor, i.e., there was no declaration of the subordination of Nepal and

5 Leo E. Rose, *Nepal: Strategy For Survival,* Berkeley: University of California Press, 1971, p. 117.

6 Kanchanmoy Mojumdar, *Political Relations Between India and Nepal 1877-1923,* New Delhi: Munshiram Manoharlal, 1973, p. 169.

Tibet to China[7]. Moreover, the words "of our own free will and choice" used in the preamble of the treaty of 1856 by Nepal clearly establishes Nepal's intention to remain a sovereign nation. The words "As before" and "shall continue to be regarded with respect"[8] can possibly be explained in two ways. If they are taken to refer to the terms of the agreement of 1792, then they are based on a document which had become a dead letter already and could not form the basis of future guidance. As already noted, both in letter and spirit, the agreement of 1792 gave no suzerain rights to China, and as such, no such rights can be relegated to the treaty of 1856 from these words. If these words are taken to describe the actual political relations existing between the two governments just before the conclusion of this treaty of 1856, it must be acknowledged that there were no signs of Nepal's vassalage to China.

The other basis of the Chinese claims was the custom of sending the quinquennial mission from Nepal to China, which continued up to 1906. The Chinese claimed that to be a tribute carrying mission to China under Article 2 of the agreement of 1792, and therefore implied the continued vassalage of Nepal to China from 1792 onwards. As one account based on Chinese sources puts it: ".... It was stipulated that Nepal's tribute status was to be like that of various other "dependents" of China, such as Korea, Annam, Siam and Burma...."[9]. Nepal, on the other hand, never regarded that as an indication of her acceptance of Chinese suzerainty, and regarded it merely as a diplomatic mission from one sovereign government to another, carrying

7 C.U. Aitchison, *A Collection of Treaties, Engagements and Sanads Relating to India and Neighbouring Countries*, Vol. XIV, New Delhi: Central Publishing Branch , 1929, pp. 49-50

8 Perceval Landon, *Nepal*, Vol. I, Kathmandu: Ratna Pustak Bhandar, Reprint, 1987, p. 282.

9 Cammann, f.n. no. 1, p. 131.

friendly gifts (and not tributes) from Nepal and bringing back similar presents from the Chinese Emperor[10].

The mission had commercial aspects. Chandra Shamsher, the Nepalese Prime Minister, had referred to this aspect to the British[11]. The Missions had provided wonderful opportunities for trade, especially from 1852 to 1900. The principal item of trade was the precious opium, which the mission took to China under diplomatic immunity. It is to be noted that the families of the then ruling elites of Nepal, including that of the Premier, were involved in this narcotic trade. Perhaps one of the main reasons behind the missions to China was the successful nature of their commercial speculations. However, it appears from the conversation between *Kazi* Bhairab Bahadur Gadhatola, the leader of the 1906 mission and J.N. Jordan, the British Minister in Peking, that by the turn of the century the Chinese had imposed severe restrictions on the sale of opium. The leader of the 1906 mission made a prophetic remark that the future Nepalese missions to China would be of doubtful utility[12]. His words came true and Nepal abolished the system of sending quinquennial missions to China after 1906.

Here it can be argued that even if we accept China's view that sending of missions by the Nepalese was a token of "their desire to be included amongst" the Chinese Emperor's "tributaries", how shall we look at the case of Tibet, which had agreed to pay Rs. 50,000 as an annual tribute to Nepal in accordance with Nepalese-Tibetan Treaty concluded with the consent of the Chinese authorities in 1790. Later, Tibet sent

---

10 Tirtha Raj Tuladhar, *Nepal-China: A Story of Friendship*, Kathmandu: Department of Publicity and Broadcasting, Ministry of National Guidance, His Majesty's Government, Nepal, 1961, p. 8.

11 Chandra Shamsher to J. Manners Smith, 19 April 1906, Foreign Sec. E, June 1906, Nos. 241-45, National Archives of India, New Delhi (NAI)

12 J.N. Jardon to Earl of Minto, 5 June 1908, Foreign Sec. E, October 1908, No. 709, NAI.

annual tributes to Nepal regularly until as late as 1953 in accordance with the treaty of 1856 between her and Nepal. Was then Tibet to be considered as a tributary or feudatory to Nepal ?

One significant point that should be mentioned is that the presents which the mission carried for the Chinese court were always described in the accompanying letter as "*Mamuli Saugat*" which means ordinary presents and not tributes[13]. It may also be added that the present, in order to be a tribute, must be fixed in cash or kind, as in the case of Tibet paying Rs 10,000 as annual tribute to Nepal. The agreement of 1792, on the other hand, stipulates only "some produce of land" which, in value, varied from one mission to another. In fact, return gifts from China were always of much more value. Furthermore, China gave top priority to Nepalese missions. All the expenses of the Nepalese mission were paid by the Chinese exchequer. The Nepalese mission was escorted by a Chinese officer whose chief duty was to provide all the comforts needed by the mission[14]

Interestingly enough, Nepal did not rigorously follow the timetable of the quinquennial missions. Although she sent missions to China regularly from 1792 to 1852, some of them went only up to the Nepal-Tibet border to submit presents there. After 1852 Nepal discontinued the quinquennial missions several times, but each time the reason for the discontinuance was clarified not by the Nepalese but by the Chinese[15]. After 1906 Nepal abolished the system unilaterally.

---

13 Chandra Shamsher to J. Manners Smith, 19 April 1906, Foreign Sec. E, June 1906, Nos. 241-245, NAI.

14 Captain Orfeur Cavenagh, *Rough Notes on the State of Nepal :· Its Government, Army and Resources*, Calcutta: W. Palmer Military Orphan Press, 1851, p. 64.

15 Tri Ratna Manandhar and Tirtha Prasad Mishra, *Nepal's Quinquennial Missions To China*, Kathmandu: Mrs. Purna Devi Manandhar and Mrs. Puspa Mishra, 1986, p. 68.

Finally it can be concluded that the political significance of the quinquennial ("tribute"?) missions has been misinterpreted generally. While they do signify the existence of close ties between the two dynasties, possibly best defined as an alliance, both Chinese and Nepalese records of that period and throughout the nineteenth century provide ample proof that the mission system did not entail Nepal's political subordination to China.

The other reason why China considered Nepal to be a tributary state was due to the acceptance of Chinese titles, robes and honours by the Nepalese Kings and the Prime Ministers. Here it should be noted that only at one time, in 1790, was King Rana Bahadur Shah of Nepal decorated with the Chinese title of 'Ertini Wang'[16]. The later rulers of Nepal were not formally decorated with this Chinese title, though the Nepalese monarchs used the term *'Wang'* for themselves while addressing the Chinese Emperors, and the latter also continued to follow the same style in their letters to the former (Nepalese monarchs). The case of the Nepalese Prime Ministers, however, was different. From the time of Jang Bahadur, especially the Nepalese Prime Ministers received the Chinese title, *"Thong Ling Pimma Ko Kang Wang Shang'* [17], and a Chinese mission regularly visited Kathmandu to decorate the new Prime Minister of Nepal with this Chinese title and the robes connected with it. It was, however, only in the first decade of the twentieth century that Nepal became aware of the fact that the Chinese titles and honours, of which she was so fond and proud, really implied, at least from the Chinese perspective, i.e. China's suzerainty over Nepal. The Nepalese denied that the Chinese titles for the Nepalese Kings and Prime Ministers in any way

---

16 Patent of 5th March 1790, J.N. Jordan to Viceroy of India, 7 March 1911, Foreign Sec. E, July 1911, No. 264, NAI.

17 R.C. Lawrence to Secretary, Govt. of India, 22 May 1871, Foreign Department Polt. A, July 1871, No. 100, NAI.

indicated Nepal's feudatory status *vis-a-vis* China[18]. Here it should be pointed out that even after Nepal stopped sending its quinquennial missions to Peking, after 1906, China continued to send ceremonial robes and titles to the new Nepalese Prime Ministers. The Nationalist Government of China had sent missions in 1930, 1932, 1934, and 1946 to confer the Chinese titles. The missions were welcomed and the titles gladly accepted by Nepal. As such, it seems that those Chinese titles and honours had only a formal value[19]. It satisfied China's ego, but on the otherhand, it added to the prestige of the Rana Prime Ministers of Nepal. Since some of them won power by force, they may have hoped to strengthen their position by receiving the stamp of approval from a ruler whose name still carried great prestige. Hence it is illogical to treat Nepal as a feudatory state of China merely on the grounds that the Nepalese Prime Ministers were decorated with Chinese titles. As regards the Chinese title awarded to the Nepalese King, it has been already mentioned that Rana Bahadur Shah was the only Nepalese monarch to get it. On the basis of this solitary evidence, Nepal cannot be categorised as a state under the suzerainty of China.

Another argument given to establish Chinese overlordship over Nepal is that the language of the Nepalese communications to the Chinese court had the style and diction of a subordinate court. As regards to this, the Nepalese Prime Minister Chandra Shamsher explained that "the customary letter which is sent on the occasion (of the quinquennial mission) is written in the truly oriental style of exuberant but meaningless politeness and follows a stereotyped rule"[20]. Here it will be helpful to recollect the story of Lord Macartney's visit to

---

18 Chandra Shamsher to J. Manners Smith, 19 November 1910, Foreign Sec. E, January 1911, No. 178, NAI.

19 Satish Kumar, "Nepal and China", *The Indian Journal of Political Science*, Vol. XXIV, No. 1, January-March 1963, p. 81.

20 Chandra Shamsher to J. Manners Smith, 19 April 1906, Foreign Sec. E, June 1906, No. 243, NAI.

Peking, carrying with him, as a matter of courtesy, a large number of presents from George III in token of King of England's goodwill towards the Emperor of China. In the Imperial decree of 4 February 1796, Emperor Ch'ien Lung, while acknowledging the gift of the English King, disclaimed any regard for the English "tribute", though valuing "the humble spirit which offers it". Ch'ien Lung said in his letter to George III, "commending your humble loyalty to our Celestial Dynasty, we now present you with further gifts and command you to display energy and dutiful loyalty so as to deserve our perpetual favour"[21]. Here it can be argued that if Nepal could be treated as a tributary to China on the basis of the language of Chinese decrees, England must also be treated as tributary to China. It is to be noted that by the close of 1910, Nepal did change her style of expression to the Chinese Emperor[22]. The wording became less submissive and humble in tone. One important point should be noted that the Chinese *Ambans* in Tibet, on receiving the Nepali text of the letter, used to translate it into Chinese, using the extravagant honorific forms considered to be appropriate by the Peking court[23]. Here it can be argued that the Nepalese submissive expressions to the Chinese Emperor did not symbolize a feudatory status, but that it was a purely complimentary style of expression.

By 1910, due to apprehension of British activity in Tibet, for the first time the Chinese formally asserted their claim of suzerainty over Nepal before the outside world. This claim was proved baseless through a challenge from both the Nepalese and the British Indian Government. The British Government found the Nepalese Government's total refutation and vehement

---

21 See Despatches from Her Britannic Majesty's Minister at Peking, 7 March 1911 and J.N. Jordan to Viceroy to India, 7 March 1911, Foreign Sec. E, July 1911, No. 264, NAI.

22 J. Manners Smith to Secretary, Govt. of India, 11 August - 12 August 1910, Foreign Sec. E, No. 115, NAI.

23 Rose, f.n. no. 5, p. 146

contradictions of all Chinese claims in this regard to be strong enough. The British Government had guaranteed Nepal's interests in Tibet, which were under direct threat from Chinese subversion. Moreover, Nepal was her ally and any encroachment upon her freedom, sovereignty and integrity by China would have adverse repercussions in the area. Therefore, the British Government conveyed to China her rejection of the Chinese claims, as well as her determination to check any attempt on the part of China to enforce 'her suzerainty' over Nepal[24]. The Chinese Government also tried to exert her best efforts on the diplomatic front to support her claim. The diplomatic tussle lasted for some time. In the meantime, the Revolution of 1911 provided the final blow to the Chinese position in Nepal, for 1911 was the year for sending the quinquennial mission to China according to the old tradition, but the British Government advised the Nepalese Government to postpone it due to the particular meaning attached to it by China. The Nepalese Government willingly accepted the advice[25]. The practice of sending Nepalese quinquennial missions to China has since been discontinued.

Meanwhile, China experienced an internal revolution which resulted in the overthrow of the Manchu dynasty and the establishment of the Republic of China under Sun Yat Sen. The fall of the Manchus, it could be argued, had freed the Nepalese Government from the obligation to send the quinquennial missions, but the significant point to be noted is that China did not give up her claim of suzerainty over Nepal. In 1913, the newly established government of the Republic of China sought to take Nepal into China's grip by asking the Nepalese to join the "Republic of five affiliated Races" (Chinese, Tibetans,

24 J.N. Jordan to Prince Ch'ing, 17 January 1911, Foreign Sec. E, July 1911, No. 258, NAI.

25 For details, See Nepalese Quinquennial Mission To China, Foreign Sec. E, February 1912, Nos. 60-71, NAI.

Mongols, Manchus, Muslims) and even offered to name Nepal as "Nepalese China"[26]. But the Nepalese Government rejected the idea altogether[27]. In 1916, Sun Yat Sen, the founder of Chinese Republic, citing a long list of so-called lost Chinese territories, including Nepal, noted that he would reclaim them[28]. In 1924, in reply to an enquiry by Perceval Landon about the Chinese attitude towards the quinquennial mission from Nepal, Dr. Wellington Koo (Ku Wai-chun), the Chinese Foreign Minister, wrote that though formerly the "tribute" came from Nepal once in five years, it was later on agreed that it should come once in twelve years. Though the new agreement referred to by the Chinese Foreign Minister was a fictitious one, it shows that China had no intention of giving up her claim over Nepal[29]. The last Chinese attempt to revive their claim over Nepal was made by Mao Tse-Tung in 1939[30]. Such a claim has not been repeated since then, as it does not seem possible for China in the present international context. Moreover, relations between Nepal and China have been strengthened through various treaties concluded between the two since 1956.

Here it would not be out of context to make an examination of the actual political status of Nepal *vis-a-vis* China. Suzerainty was originally an institution of feudal law and was used to describe the particular relationship between the feudal lord and his vassal. The latter owed allegiance to the

---

26 General Chung to the *Maharaja* of Nepal, 23 February 1913, Foreign Dept. Sec. External, August 1913, No. 240, NAI.

27 Chandra Shamsher to General Chung, 16 March 1913, Foreign Dept. Sec. External, August 1913, No. 248, NAI.

28 Poorna Bahadur M.A., *Nepal Behind the Screen*, Kathmandu: Nepal Youth League, Central Committee, 1957, pp. 15-16, and Ashok Kumar Nigam, "Chinese Claim of Suzerainty over Nepal", *The Modern Review*, Calcutta, September 1968, p. 681.

29 Perceval Landon, *Nepal*, Vol. II, Kathmandu: Ratna Pustak Bhandar, Reprint, 1987, p. 103.

30 Girilal Jain, *India Meets China in Nepal*, Bombay: Asia Publishing House, 1959, pp. 106-107.

suzerain ruler, he had to pay his tribute, had to give him his military support, and in return was entitled to his protection. As to the paying of any 'tribute', it has already been discussed how the Chinese on their part have tried to interpret the wording of Article 2 of the agreement of 1792 and the sending of Nepalese quinquennial missions to China as an arrangement for paying 'tribute' to her. It should be pointed out that Nepal never gave any military support to China. Nepalese (Gurkha) soldiers, on the contrary, were sent with the consent of the Nepalese Government to fight for the British against the Chinese in the Boxer Uprising of 1900-1901[31]. Again in 1903-1904, Nepal gave all its support to the British expedition against Tibet, which was claimed by China to be her vassal and as such, a part of her territory. These instances negate the very idea of any "allegiance" on the part of Nepal towards China. Besides that, China never tried to represent Nepal in her relations with other nations, though she had tried to do so in the case of Tibet. Nepal neither fought any war by the side of China nor was any treaty concluded by China ever deemed to be binding in Nepal. In fact, Nepal was more inclined to side with the British India Government in the international sphere, and sometimes even fought wars side by side with the British Government.

Moreover, Nepal has been declaring wars and concluding all types of treaties without outside participation. This in itself is a sufficient proof of Nepal's sovereignty. Nepal always signed all types of treaties in her own independent capacity, sometimes even prejudicial to Chinese interests. China, though having a full knowledge of affairs, never interfered with or objected to these actions on the part of Nepal. This unfettered activity throughout the history well establishes her sovereignty.

---

31 Francis Tuker, *Gorkha: The Story of The Gurkhas of Nepal*, London: Constable and Co., 1957, p. 192

That Peking has drawn a clear distinction between the respective positions of Nepal and Tibet *vis-a-vis* China is clearly evident in Chinese official documents. Throughout the nineteenth century, Chinese officials, in their reports on developments in the Himalayan area, usually classified Nepal as belonging within the broad framework of the British Imperialist system in India. In 1860, the Chinese government, in an Imperial decree published in the Peking Gazette, described Nepal as "a small country and a poor one. More than this, it is subject to the Pe-L'ing (English) barbarians"[32]. In the case of Tibet, matters like the appointment of a permanent Chinese *Amban* in Tibet and his repeated efforts to interfere with the external and internal affairs of the state, as well as Chinese insistence on not allowing any treaty with Tibet to become valid if it had neither been concluded nor approved by her, made Tibet's independent status controversial. Nothing of the sort is to be found in her relations with Nepal. A Chinese garrison was stationed in Tibet, whereas China had no such garrison posted in Nepal. The Chinese *Amban* in Tibet, in times of need, acted only as an "Ambassador" (and not a resident) to advise the Nepalese Government and mediate between the Governments of China and Nepal. Besides, Nepal was keeping its representative at the status of a *Vakil*(envoy) at Lhasa, Tibet's capital, which would not have been possible had she been a tributary to China.

Finally the question then arises as to what was the real political status of Nepal *vis-a-vis* China ? The Chinese claim of suzerainty over Nepal is indeed difficult to assess from the western point of view. It was often a matter of symbolic rather than substantive right. Here it should be noted that in the Imperial Dynastic Chronicles a large number of European, Asian and African countries were listed as "tributaries" of China, but about most of them the Chinese Government had no

---

32 Asad Husain, *British India's Relations With the Kingdom of Nepal,* London: George Allen and Unwin Ltd., 1970, p. 266.

adequate knowledge, let alone any regular intercourse with them. These states were "tributaries" of China in the sense that from the Chinese point of view, any foreign state having any relationship or intercourse with China was a tributary[33]. The Chinese regarded themselves as a superior people and all others as barbarians. During that period, trade with China was a highly prized object for the foreign states to whom the Chinese Government granted commercial facilities upon the acceptance of China's cultural superiority. The tribute relations were, from the traditional Chinese point of view, only a type of foreign relations and commercial transactions. As such, it is quite difficult to interpret the Chinese tributary system from the western point of view, and in terms taken from the western political vocabulary. Suzerainty, from the western point of view, has primarily a political connotation-- (a) a suzerain not only claims but exercises exclusive political influence on the feudatory, and (b) a suzerain has the corresponding obligation for the latter's defence against external threat. China's tributary system in relation to Nepal, on the other hand, involved neither exclusive political influence nor any responsibility to defend Nepal from the British attack like that of 1814-1816.

In the final analysis it can be stated that Nepal's so-called "tributary" relationship with China, from the political and legal point of view, seemed less real and more psychological. The quinquennial mission was sent less as an acknowledgement of subjection than as a token of compliment, amity and deference to a time-honoured relation, and as a convenient means of making a profitable commercial transaction. Nepal's continued respect and signs of gratitude to the Chinese Emperor as a father-figure stemmed from her desire to balance herself against British India. Nepal was always very

---

33 J.K. Fairbank and S.Y. Teng, "On the Ch'ing Tributary System", *Harvard Journal of Asiatic Studies,* Vol. VI, 1941, pp. 135-246.

keen to maintain the traditional relations with China, because even her acceptance of the Emperor as a father-figure did not mean losing her sovereignty (gave her full independence) while her nearness to British India did not mean total subjugation. Thus, has the labelling of the political status of Nepal *vis-a-vis* China as a suzerain-vassalage relationship still any grounds for justification ?

***

Selected Bibliography

Primary Sources

Unpublished Documents

National Archives of India, New Delhi:

'Nepalese Embassy to China', Foreign Secret Consultation, 26 May 1854, Nos. 50-53.

'Khilluts for the Nipal Durbar from the Emperor of China', Foreign Secret Consultation, 27 August 1858, No. 96.

'Intention of Nipalese Government to resume diplomatic relations with Court of Pekin', Foreign Political A, June 1866, Nos. 163-164.

'Reports the Starting of the Mission to Pekin with presents for the Emperor', Foreign Political A, August 1866, No. 104.

'Nepalese Embassy to China', Foreign Political A, August 1867, Nos. 53-54.

'Countries traversed by the late Nepalese Mission to China', Foreign Secret I, September 1870, Nos. 400-404.

'Visit of a Chinese Mission to Nepal', Foreign Political A, July 1871, Nos. 100-105.

'Alleged Illicit traffic in opium through Nepal', Foreign Political A, May 1875, Nos. 104-104A.

'Embassy from Nipal to China', Foreign Secret, September 1876, Nos. 129-133.

'Nepalese "tribute" mission to China', Foreign Secret, October 1877, Nos. 149-150.

'Chinese Title Conferred upon Maharaja Ranudip Singh', Foreign Political A, February 1878, Nos. 178-183.

'Nepalese Mission to China', Foreign Secret, December 1878, Nos. 23-28.

'Nipalese Mission to China', Foreign Secret, June 1879, Nos. 22-25.

'Arrival in Peking of a Mission from Nipal', Foreign Political A, April 1880, Nos. 98-99.

'Departure of the Nipalese Mission', Foreign Political A, January 1881, Nos. 83-84.

'Departure of the usual Comp'imentary Nepalese Misison to Pekin', Foreign Secret E., October 1886, Nos. 1-2.

'Intention of the Nepal Darbar to despatch the usual Complimentary Mission to Peking', Foreign Secret E, July 1894, Nos. 184-185.

'Return to Nepal of the Quinquennial Mission to China', Foreign External B, April 1901, No. 31.

'Affairs in Nepal', Foreign Secret E, September 1902, Nos. 127-133.

'Itinerary of Kazi Indra Bikram Rana from Kathmandu to Peking in Samvat 1951', Foreign Secret E, September 1904, Nos. 88-97.

'Nepalese Commercial Mission to China', Foreign Secret E, June 1906, Nos. 241-245.

'Nepalese Commercial Mission to China', Foreign Secret E, September 1906, Nos. 262-265.

'Action of the Chinese in Tibet', Foreign Secret E, May 1907, Nos. 181-279.

'News-Letters from the Nepalese Representative at Lhasa regarding Tibet Affairs', Foreign Secret E, June 1907, Nos. 76-102.

'Nepalese Commercial Mission to China', Foreign Secret E, July 1907, Nos. 304-305.

'Nepalese Commercial Mission to China', Foreign Secret E, September 1907, Nos. 98-99.

'Transmission through H.B. M.'s Minister Peking of a cover containing a draft for 2029 Taels for delivery to Her Officer in charge of the Nepalese Mission to Peking', Foreign External B, January 1908, Nos. 92-95.

'Nepalese Commercial Mission to Peking', Foreign Secret E, March 1908, Nos. 1-7.

'Nepalese Commercial Mission to China', Foreign Secret E, October 1908, Nos. 696-717.

'Departure of the Nepalese Commercial Mission from Peking', Foreign Secret E, January 1909, Nos. 411-413.

'Report regarding the Nepalese Commercial Mission to China', Foreign Secret E, June 1909, Nos. 478-482.

'Nepalese Mission to China and Thanks of the Nepal Durbar to British Consuls for their Kindness and Courtesy to the Mission', Foreign Secret E, September 1909, Nos. 16-21.

Nepalese Commercial Mission to China', Foreign Secret E, October 1909, Nos. 713-716.

Action of the Chinese in Tibet and the Flight of the Dalai Lama to India', Foreign Secret E., March 1910, Nos. 385-510.

'Chinese Claims to Suzerainty over Nepal and Bhutan and Report that Chinese Envoys are to be despatched to the Maharaja of Bhutan and the Prime Minister of Nepal giving to each a letter and title from the Chinese

Emperor', Foreign Secret E, January 1911, Nos. 124-207.

'Rejection of Chinese Claims to Suzerainty over Nepal and Bhutan', Foreign Secret E, July 1911, Nos. 248-280.

'Employment by the Chinese of Ex-Gurkha Soldiers of the Indian Army as Instructors in their own army', Foreign External B, Septermber 1911, No. 94.

'Employment by the Chinese of Ex-Gurkha Soldiers of the Indian Army as Drill Instructors', Foreign External B, January 1912, No. 730.

'Nepalese Quinquennial Mission to China', Foreign Secret E., February 1912, Nos. 60-70.

'Chinese Intrigues with Nepal', Foreign Secret E, August 1913, Nos. 240-250.

Ministry of Foreign Affairs, Kathmandu:

'Documents dealing with different aspects of Nepalese History from 1837 to 1959', E[1] Poka No. 15.

'Documents dealing with Nepalese Quinquennial Missions to China', Poka No. 64.

'Documents relating to Nepal-Tibet and China Relations', Unnumbered Poka.

National Archives of Nepal, Kathmandu:

'Documents dealing with bestowing of Chinese title to Dev Shamsher', Poka No. 2, Letter No. 141

'Documents relating to bestowing of Chinese title and robes to Bir Shamsher', Poka No. 2, Letter No. 142.

Royal Nepal Army Head-Quarters Kathmandu:

'Documents relating to presents sent to the Chinese and Tibetan authorities through the Nepalese missions', Part 3, Serial No. 63 (53).

Published Document (English)

Aitchison, C.U., *A Collection of Treaties, Engagements and Sanads Relating to India and Neighbouring Countries*, Vol. XIV, New Delhi: Central Publishing Branch, 1929.

Published Documents (Nepali)

"Nepal Desh Ko Itihas" (History of Nepal), A Manuscript in the National Archives of Nepal, Kathmandu, Published in *Ancient Nepal*, No. 27, April, 1974.

Naraharinath, Yogi (ed.), *Itihas Prakash* (Lights on History), Part I and II, Kathmandu: Nepal Press, 2012 B.S.

Secondary Sources

Books in English

Bagchi, Prabodh Chandra, *India and China: A Thousand Years of Cultural Relations*, New York: Philosophical Library, 1951.

Bapat, P.V. (ed.), *2500 Years of Buddhism*, Delhi: The Publications Division, Ministry of Information and Broadcasting, Government of India, 1959.

Bell, Charles, *Tibet: Past and Present*, Delhi: Motilal Banarsidass Publishers Pvt. Ltd., Reprint, 1992.

Cammann, Schuyler, *Trade through the Himalayas*, Princeton, New Jersey: Princeton University Press, 1951.

Cavenagh, Captain Orfeur, *Rough Notes on the State of Nepal: Its Governments, Army and Resources*, Calcutta: W. Palmer Military Orphan Press. 1851.

Ch'en, Kenneth K.S., *Buddhism in China: A Historical Survey*, Princeton New Jersey: Princeton, University Press, 1964.

Das, Sarat Chandra, *Indian Pandits in the Land of Snow*, Calcutta: Firma K.L. Mukhopadhyay, Reprint, 1965.

Fairbank, John K. (ed.), *The Chinese World Order*, Cambridge, Massachusetts: Harvard University Press, 1970.

Fergusson, W.N., *Land and People of Tibet and China in the Early Twentieth Century*, Delhi: Sharda Prakashan, Reprint, 1989.

Fisher, Margaret W. and Rose, Leo E., *England, India, Nepal, Tibet, China 1765-1958*, Berkeley: University of California, 1959.

Ghoble, T.R., *China-Nepal Relations and India*, New Delhi: Deep and Deep Publications, 1986.

Husian, Asad. *British India's Relations with the Kingdom of Nepal*, London : George Allen and Unwin Ltd., 1970.

Jain, Girilal, *India Meets China in Nepal*, Bombay: Asia Publishing House, 1959.

K.C., Kaisher Bahadur, *Nepal After the Revolution of 1950*, Vol. I, Kathmandu: Sharada Prakashan Griha, 1976.

K.C., Keshar Bahadur, *The Judicial Customs of Nepal*, Part I, Kathmandu: Ratna Pustak Bhandar, 1971.

Kirkpatrick, Colonel, *An Account of the Kingdom of Nepaul*, New Delhi: Asian Educational Services, Reprint, 1986.

Lamb, Alastair, *The Mac Mohan Line*, Vol. II, London: Routledge and Kegan Paul, 1966.

Lamb, Alastair, *Tibet, China & India 1914-1950*, Hertfordshire: Roxford Books, 1989.

Landon, Perceval, *Nepal*, 2 Vols., Kathmandu: Ratna Pustak Bhandar, Reprint, 1987.

M.A., Poorna Bahadur, *Nepal Behind The Screen*, Kathmandu: Nepal Youth League Central Committee, 1957.

Majumdar, R.C., *The Classical Age*, Bombay: Bharatiya Vidya Bhawan, 1962.

Manandhar, Tri Ratna, *Some Aspects of Rana Rule in Nepal*, Kathmandu: Purna Devi Manandhar, 1983.

Manandhar, Tri Ratna, *Nepal: The Years of Trouble (1877-85)*, Kathmandu: Purna Devi Manandhar, 1986.

Manandhar, Tri Ratna and Mishra, Tirtha Prasad, *Nepal's Quinquennial Missions to China*, Kathmandu: Mrs. Purna Devi Manandhar and Mrs. Puspa Mishra, 1986.

Mojumdar, Kanchanmoy, *Anglo-Nepalese Relations in the Nineteenth Century,* Calcutta: Firma K.L. Mukhopadhyay, 1973.

Mojumdar, Kanchanmoy, *Political Relations Between India and Nepal 1877-1923,* New Delhi: Munshiram Manoharlal Publishers Pvt. Ltd., 1973.

Nariman, J.K., *Literary History of Sanskrit Buddhism*, Delhi: Motilal Banarsidass. Reprint, 1972.

Nehru, Jawaharlal, *The Discovery of India*, London: Meridian Books Limited, 1960.

Prasad, Ishwari, *The Life and Times of Maharaja Juddha Shumsher Jung Bahadur Rana of Nepal*, New Delhi: Ashish Publishing House, 1975.

Rana, Pudma Jung Bahadur, *Life of Maharaja Sir Jung Bahadur*, Kathmandu: Ratna Pustak Bhandar, Reprint, 1980.

Regmi, D.R., *Modern Nepal*, Vol. I, Calcutta: Firma K.L. Mukhopadhayay, 1975.

Richardson, H.E., *Tibet and Its History*, London: Oxford University Press, 1962.

Rose, Leo E., *Nepal : Strategy For Survival*, Berkeley: University of California Press, 1971.

Sen, Jahar, *Indo-Nepal Trade in the Nineteenth Century*, Calcutta: Firma KLM Pvt. Ltd., 1977.

Sever, Adrian, *Nepal Under the Ranas*, New Delhi: Oxford and IBH Publishing Co. Pvt. Ltd., 1993.

Sever, Adrian, *Aspects of Modern Nepalese History,* New Delhi: Vikas Publishing House Pvt. Ltd., 1996.

Shaha, Rishikesh, *Heroes and Builders of Nepal*, London: Oxford University Press, 1965.

Shaha, Rishikesh, *Modern Nepal: A Political History 1885-1955*, Vol. II, New Delhi: Manohar Publications, 1990.

Shakabpa, Tsepon W.D., *Tibet: A Political History*, New Heaven: Yale University, 1967.

Tikhvinsky, S.L. (ed.), *China and Her Neighbours: From Ancient Times to the Middle Ages*, Moscow: Progress Publishers, 1981.

Tucci, Giuseppe, *The Religions of Tibet*, New Delhi: Allied Publishers Private Limited, 1980.

Tuker, Francis, *Gorkha: The Story of the Gurkhas of Nepal*, London : Constable and Company Ltd., 1957.

Tuladhar, Tirtha R., *Nepal-China: A Story of Friendship*, Kathmandu: Department of Publicity and Broadcasting, Ministry of National Guidance, His Majesty's Government, Nepal, 1961.

Twitchett, Dennis and Fairbank, John K. (General Editors), *The Cambridge History of China*, Vol. 10, Late Ch'ing 1800-1911, Part I, Cambridge: Cambridge University Press, 1978.

Uprety, Prem R., *Nepal-Tibet Relations 1850-1930*, Kathmandu: Puga Nara, 1980.

Van Walt Van Praag, Michael C., *The Status of Tibet*, Boulder, Colorado: West View Press, 1987.

Welch, Holmes, *Buddhism Under Mao*, Cambridge, Massachusetts: Harvard University Press, 1972.

Wright, Daniel (ed.), *History of Nepal Translated From Parbatiya*, Calcutta: Susil Gupta (India) Private Ltd., Second Edition, 1958.

Zurcher, E., *The Buddhist Conquest of China*, 2 Vols., Leiden: E.J. Brill, 1972.

Books in Nepali

Bhattarai, Niranjan, *Chin Ra Tyasasita Nepal Ko Sambandha*, (China and Her Relations with Nepal), Kathmandu: Royal Nepal Academy, 2018 B.S.

Joshi, Satya Mohan, *Kalakar Arniko* (Architect Arniko), Kathmandu: Bijay Gajananda Vaidya, 2044 B.S.

Nepal, Jnanmani, *Nepal Nirukta* (Nepal Identified), Kathmandu: Royal Nepal Academy, 2041 B.S.

Nepal, Jnanmani, *Nepal-Bhot Chin Sambandhaka Kehi Sanskritik Paksha* (Some Cultural Aspect of Nepal-Tibet China Relations), Kathmandu: Royal Nepal Academy, 2045 B.S.

Rana, Purushottam Shamsher Jang Bahadur, *Sri Tin Haruko Tathya Brittanta* (Factual Description of Sri Tins), Banaras: Parambir Shamsher J.B.R., 2047 B.S.

Books in Hindi

Sanskrityan, Rahul, *Baudha Sanskriti* (Buddhist Culture), Calcutta: Adhunik Pustak Bhawan, no date.

Upadhyaya, Bhagwatsharan, *Brihattar Bharat* (Greater India), Delhi: Rajpal and Sons, 1986.

Book in Nepal Bhasa (Newari)

Shrestha, Swayambhu Lal, *Swayambhu Lal Shresthaya Layaya Chowkhan* (Selected Essays of Swayambhu Lal Shrestha on Nepalese Culture), Part I, Lalitpur: Lok Sahitya Parishad, Nepal Sambat 1106 (2043 B.S.)

Articles (English)

Fairbank, John K. and Teng, S.Y., "On the Ch'ing Tributary System", *Harvard Journal of Asiatic Studies*, Vol. VI, 1941.

K.C., Keshar Bahadur, "Historical Analysis with translations into English of the Bi-Lingual inscription of 'A'rya Usnisa Vijaya Dharani' Discovered by His Majesty King Mahendra in the Museum of Sian on Friday, October 6, 1961". *Souvenir*, Kathmandu: Nepal-China Cultural Council, 1982.

Kumar, Satish, "Nepal and China", *The Indian Journal of Political Science,* Vol. XXIV, No. 1, January-March 1963.

Manandhar, Vijay Kumar, "*Sahu* Dharma Narayan Manandhar: A Financier And Member of the Bureaucratic Elite of the Nineteenth Century", *Voice of History,* Vol. XIV, No. 1 (June 1999), pp. 19-36.

Nigam, Ashok Kumar, "Chinese Claim of Suzerainty over Nepal", *The Modern Review,* Calcutta, September 1968.

Rose, Leo E, "Sino-Indian Rivalry and the Himalayan Border States", *Orbis*, Vol. V, No. 2, July 1961, The Quarterly Journal of World Affairs, University of Pennsylvania.

Uprety, Prem, "Honors, Medals and Honorific Titles: An Understanding into the Nepali Historical Past", *Tribhuvan University Journal,* Vol. XVIII, June 1995.

Articles (Nepali)

Dhúngel, Ramesh, "Aitihasik Chinia Padak-Thong Lin Pimma Kokang Wang Syan" (Historical Chinese Title-Thong Lin Pimma Kokang Wang Syan), *Smarika* (Souvenir), Nos. 4-5, Kathmandu: Nepal-China Friendship Association, 2043 B.S.

Dixit, Kamalmani, "Batha Matrai Hun Ki?" (Was Clever only?), *Nepali*, Nepali Quarterly, No. 98, Magh 2040 B.S.

Karki, Durga Devi, "Aitihasik Shrota Ra Shrotako Rupma Antarbaarta" (Historical Source and Interview as Source), *Rolamba*, Vol. 9, No. 1, January-March, 1989.

Mishra, Tirtha Prasad, "Sri Tin Maharaj Chandra Shamsher Ra Chinia Sammaan" (Prime Minister Chandra Shamsher and Chinese Honour), *Ancient Nepal*, Journal of the Department of Archaeology, Kathmandu, Nos. 98-99, February-May 1987.

Nepal, Jnanmani, "Jang Bahadur Ko Bidesh Niti Ra Sambat 1904 Ko Pechin Jane Pratinidhi Mandal" (Jang Bahadur's Foreign Policy and Mission to Peking of 1904 B.S.), *Contributions to Nepalese Studies*, Journal of Centre for Nepal and Asian Studies, Tribhuvan University, Kathmandu, Vol. VIII, No. 2, June 1981.

Nepali, ChittaRanjan, "Nepal-Chin Yuddha" (Nepal-China War), *Sharada*, Vol. 21, No. 1, 2013 B.S.

Article (Nepal Bhasa or Newari)

Manandhar, Jit Bahadur, "Dhamana Sayami", *Smarika* (Souvenir) Published by Kendriya Manandhar Sangha

(Centr..! Manandhar Association), 1115 Nepal Sambat (2051 B.S.).

Published Books and Articles (Oriental)

Beal, Samuel, *Buddhist Records of the Western World*, Delhi: Oriental Book Reprint Corporation, Reprint, 1983.

Chang, Huang Sheng, "China and Nepal", *People's China*, 1 May 1956.

Chao, Pu-Chu, *Buddhism in China*, Peking: Chinese Buddhist Association, 1957.

Chou, Hsiang-Kuang, *A History of Chinese Buddhism*, Allahabad: Indo-Chinese Literature Publication, 1956.

Fa-hsien, *A Record of the Buddhist Countries*, Peking: Chinese Buddhist Association, 1957.

Ikeda, Daisaku, *The Flower of Chinese Buddhism*, Tokyo: Whitehall, 1989.

Lee, Daniel J., "National China Re-establishes Relations with the Kingdom of Nepal", *The China Weekly Review*, Shanghai, Vol. 55, 27 December, 1930.

Lee, Daniel J., "The Prime Minister of Nepal Decorated By China", *The China Weekly Review*, Shanghai, Vol. 60, 9 April, 1932.

Lee, Jenkins, "Chinese Mission To Nepal", *The China Weekly Review*, Shanghai, Vol. 70, 17 November, 1934.

Legge, James, *A Record of Buddhistic Kingdoms: Being an account by the Chinese monk Fa-hien of his travels in India and Ceylon (A.D. 399-414) in search of the Buddhist books of discipline*, New York: Paragon Book Reprint Corp., 1965.

Levi, Sylvain, "Nepal" Translated into English, Published in *Ancient Nepal*, Journal of the Department of Archaeology, Kathmandu, No. 27, April 1974.

Martyonov, A.S., "Some Aspects of Qing Policy in Tibet at the close of the 18th Century", in S.L. Tikhvinsky (ed.), *Manzhou Rule in China*, Moscow: Progress Publishers, 1983.

Meng, C.Y.W., "China's Interest in the Complications Between Tibet and Nepal;", *The China Weekly Review*, Shanghai, 26 April, 1930.

Mu, Chin Keh, *A Short History of Sino-Indian Friendship*, Calcutta: 1981.

Parker, E.H., "Nepaul and China", *The Imperial and Asiatic Quarterly Review and Oriental and Colonial Record*, Vol. VII, 1899.

Petech, L., *Northern India according to the Shui-Ching-Chu*, Rome: Instituto Poligrafico Dello Stato Piazza Verdi, 1950.

Suzuki, Chusei, "China's Relations With Inner Asia: The Hsiung-Nu, Tibet", in John K. Fairbank (ed.), *The Chinese World Order*, Cambridge, Massachusetts: Harvard University Press, 1970.

Wang, Hung-wi, "Chin Nepal Maitri, Prachin Tara Naulo Utsah Sahitko" (Ancient China-Nepal Ties But with new enthusiasm), *Souvenir*, Kathmandu: Nepal-Chin Maitri Sangh, 2041 B.S.

Newspaper

Gorkhapatra, Nepali Weekly (Now Daily), Kathmandu, 1991 B.S. Jestha 26 (8 June, 1934).

***

Index

***